Using Voice and Song in Therapy

of related interest

Therapeutic Voicework
Principles and Practice for the Use of Singing as a Therapy
Paul Newham
ISBN 185302 361 2

Using Voice and Movement in Therapy
The Practical Application of Voice Movement Therapy
Paul Newham
ISBN 185302 592 5

Foundations of Expressive Arts Therapy
Theoretical and Clinical Perspectives
Edited by Stephen K Levine and Ellen G Levine
ISBN 1 85302 463 5

Music for Life
Aspects of Creative Music Therapy with Adult Clients
Gary Ansdell
ISBN 185302 299 3

Music Therapy in Health and Education
Edited by Margaret Heal and Tony Wigram
ISBN 185302 175 X

Music Therapy in Context
Music, Meaning and Relationship
Mercedes Pavlicevic
ISBN 185302 434 1

Music Therapy Research and Practice in Medicine
From Out of the Silence
David Aldridge
ISBN 185302 296 9

Using Voice and Song in Therapy

The Practical Application
of Voice Movement Therapy

Paul Newham

Jessica Kingsley Publishers
London and Philadelphia

The right of Paul Newham to be identified as author of this work has been asserted by him in accordance with the Copyright, Designs and Patents Act 1988.

First published in the United Kingdom in 1999 by
Jessica Kingsley Publishers Ltd
116 Pentonville Road
London N1 9JB, England
and
325 Chestnut Street,
Philadelphia, PA 19106, USA.
www.jkp.com

Copyright © 1999 Paul Newham

Library of Congress Cataloging in Publication Data
Newham, Paul, 1962–
Using voice and song in therapy : the practical application of voice movement therapy
/ Paul Newham.
p. cm.
Includes bibliographical references and index.
ISBN 1-85302-590-9 (v. 2 : pbk. : alk. paper)
1. Singing--Therapeutic use. 2. Voice--Therapeutic use.
I. Title.
RZ999.N436 1999
615.8'5154--dc21
98-50699
CIP

British Library Cataloguing in Publication Data
Newham, Paul
Using voice and song in therapy
Vol.2: The practical application of voice movement therapy
1. Singing - Therapeutic use 2.Voice - Therapeutic use
I.Title
616.8'91654
ISBN 1 85302 590 9

Printed and Bound in Great Britain by
Athenaeum Press, Gateshead, Tyne and Wear

Contents

This book is for Melanie, whose voice has inspired
tears and laughter and who knows the wounds and the
healing and all the shades between.
Her voice holds the magic of inspiration.

Voice Movement Therapy – Towards an Integrated Model of Expressive Arts Therapy

Over the past 15 years I have been developing a systematic methodology for using singing and vocalisation as a therapeutic modality. On a personal level, I think the genesis of my work originates in the acoustic cacophony of my childhood, where the angry vocal yells of my father and the sorrowful vocal cries of my mother provided the musical accompaniment to my days. On a professional level, my investigative work began with my search for a way of developing liberated vocal self-expression in people with severe mental and physical handicaps who could not speak but who produced a broad spectrum of non-verbal sounds.

Alone and without a model for what I was attempting to do, I spent many years crawling along the floor, gurgling, screeching, singing and mirroring the many sounds which my clients made in order that I might enter into their language rather than seeking to demand that they speak mine.

I found that with patience and an experimental spirit I could release a certain amount of muscular tension and facilitate a more liberated use of the voice in people whose verbal proficiency was limited or non-existent. With this vocal release my clients seemed also to access a degree of positive emotional expression and an attitude of celebration, as though a certain anguish had been assuaged. The question then was what to do with these voices which emerged.

Simultaneous with my investigations into voice with handicapped people, I was working as a composer and vocalist, drawing inspiration and influence from a multi-cultural musical perspective. As my knowledge of the world's music broadened I began to hear parallels between certain vocal qualities in indigenous singing styles, particularly those of the East and

Middle East, and the sounds made by my handicapped clients. Taking short frozen moments from a variety of singing styles and comparing them with short recordings of handicapped voices, I realised that it was often not possible to tell which was which. I then began to produce performances with my clients which choreographed their movements and orchestrated their vocal sounds to create impressionistic theatre pieces.

By combining my artistic research with a study of physiology, I began to evolve a method for using singing as a mode of artistic expression and therapeutic investigation with non-verbal populations. But the key to my work was the use of my own voice as a probe and a mirror. I learned to expand radically the tonal range and timbral malleability of my voice and use this instrument to communicate with my non-speaking clients. Though we could not speak with one another, we could sing – taking singing in its broadest sense. As my work expanded I was increasingly asked to train other professionals to make use of my methods and I gradually began to withdraw from working directly with handicapped people and started to work with professional care assistants, speech therapists, psychologists and a broad range of workers in the field of special education.

Because the exploration of my own voice had been so central to my investigations, my work with these new so-called 'able' clients took a very practical form. I offered one-to-one voice and singing lessons where the objective was not to produce a beautiful voice but to explore the complete vocal range, valuing all sounds as an authentic expression of the person. However, whereas the main obstacles to liberated vocal expression amongst my original handicapped clients had been neuromuscular, it seemed that my new clientele were inhibited and constricted primarily by psychological issues which manifested in various muscular hypertensions that inhibited and impeded liberated use of the voice. In addition, when I was able to facilitate vocal liberation, new-found sounds were often accompanied by intense emotions which in their turn produced new sounds as my clients experienced a spectrum of feelings from deep grief to tumultuous joy, expressed through vocal qualities ranging from guttural bass to piercing soprano. I therefore realised that to progress with the development of my work, I had to understand thoroughly not only the physiological nature of vocal expression but also the relationship between voice and psyche. In consequence I combined a theoretical study of physiology and psychotherapy with the undergoing of my own personal psychoanalysis.

In order to understand in more detail the physiological process of vocalisation I needed to observe the internal workings of my larynx whilst vocalising. I was therefore honoured and grateful when David Garfield-Davies, at that time consultant laryngologist at the Middlesex Hospital, London, offered to make a video stroboscopic recording of my working larynx by threading a fibre optic camera through my nasal passages. This confirmed that the techniques I was forging not only enabled the vocal instrument to increase radically tonal range and timbral malleability, but also they did so in a way entirely synonymous with healthy methods of voice production. Film of this can be seen on the accompanying video to this book *Shouting for Jericho: The Work of Paul Newham on the Human Voice* (Newham 1997). Meanwhile, I began to realise that many of the tenets of psychotherapy could be transposed from a verbal to a vocal mode of expression. I believed that I was establishing the idea of singing as therapy.

In time my one-to-one practice grew to include many other kinds of clients besides those who wanted to learn the principles of my work in order to apply it professionally. As my private practice of one-to-one voice sessions grew, I had the opportunity to apply my evolving systematic methodology of vocal work to a broad range of clients, some of whom came in the hope of alleviating physical problems such as constriction, asthma, and stammering, whilst others came for psychological reasons such as shyness, debilitating grief or repressed anger. The systematic approach which I had forged from my work with mentally and physically handicapped people was equally effective with this clientele and the added dimension of acknowledging the psychological significance of the process deepened the work with all clients.

Though each client brought with them into my consulting room unique issues which were worked through and explored not through speaking but through singing, I began to recognise certain approaches, exercises, methods and exploratory investigations which seemed to facilitate authentic vocal expression in all clients, regardless of their unique disposition.

Combining the use of my emerging system of vocal release with a unique personal psychotherapeutic relationship with each individual client I realised that I was creating the foundations for a therapeutic modality which compared to the expressive arts therapies – such as drama therapy and dance therapy – except that the channel of expression was voice and movement. I called this modality Voice Movement Therapy.

At the heart of my work was – and is – a systematic methodology for interpreting vocal sound. This system distils the voice into ten acoustic components which emanate from physiological functioning, which provide a language for describing the voice and which relate to psychological, emotional and artistic expression. This system is described in detail in my book *Therapeutic Voicework: Principles and Practice for the Use of Singing as a Therapy* (Newham 1997b) and is presented in Chapter 5 of this volume. A concise recap of the system is also outlined briefly in Appendix 1 of this volume. Because of the difficulty inherent in attempting to describe vocal sounds in written words, I have published a set of audio cassette tapes *The Singing Cure: Liberating Self Expression Through Voice Movement Therapy* (Newham 1998) which explain the Voice Movement Therapy System of Vocal Analysis, giving ample vocal examples of the spectrum of vocal sounds in speech and song which arise from different combinations of the ten core ingredients. Details of how to obtain accompanying resources to this book and access other information regarding Voice Movement Therapy are given in Appendix 2 of this volume.

Before long, I had more clients and more work than I could possibly handle. I therefore considered that I could actually reach more clients by training others to impart the work as facilitators, voice coaches, singing teachers, therapists, special education workers and community leaders; so I began running short courses in the techniques and methodologies which I had forged.

In the summer following the first series of short courses, I became unable to work due to exhaustion, and a graduate of one of my training courses, Jenni Roditi, offered to take over my client practice. Roditi did this with proficiency and skill; and in so doing she verified that the techniques were indeed grounded and practicable enough to be passed on and administered by others with equal efficacy as when administered by myself.

On returning to teaching the courses which I was developing and as I observed graduates apply the work in various settings I began to be convinced that there was a need for more trained and qualified practitioners who could use voice to facilitate a therapeutic process which yielded liberated self-expression in others. I therefore developed the short courses which I had been teaching into a full professional training leading to a professional Diploma in Voice Movement Therapy, which is currently accredited by the Oxford and Cambridge University and Royal Society of Arts Examinations Board. The major focus of my work is now directing this professional training in Voice Movement Therapy and teaching other short courses in specific areas of the work.

The professional training course in Voice Movement Therapy provides a thorough practical, experiential and technical education in an approach to working therapeutically with the voice which synthesises the physiological, artistic, psychological and educational aspects of vocal work in a single strategy. Because of its broad but integrated nature, it has attracted students from many backgrounds from all over the world. Trainees include musicians or performing artists seeking to develop their vocal and compositional skills; psychotherapists seeking to incorporate vocal work into their approach; speech and language therapists seeking an integrated and experiential model to complement their allopathic training; freelance peripatetic group leaders who run workshops and offer sessional work for a variety of client groups; and many others whose professional intention is unclear but who seek a personal vocational training which unites exploration of the Self with the acquisition of technical skills. The diverse student fraternity provides a particularly fertile environment and graduates utilise the work in very different ways. Some graduates work with clients or patients in clinical institutions or in one-to-one practice; some devise performances and lead experiential workshops; some offer vocal training in drama schools and in individual client practice; some combine the vocal work with other arts therapies or with physical therapies; and others work in a way that combines a number of different models.

Although the designing and teaching of this course in many ways provided a culmination to my intentions, there was still a missing link. For, on graduating from the training course, practitioners encounter many complex issues relating to the practice of Voice Movement Therapy for which they need further support, supervision, guidance and a sense of being part of a network. I therefore formed the International Association for Voice Movement Therapy which is governed by a Code of Ethics and a Constitution and to which qualified graduate practitioners of Voice Movement Therapy belong. This Association is in its early days but provides an entirely necessary forum for the supervision of practitioners and an investigation of issues relating to the practice of a therapeutic approach to vocal expression.

In seeking to ground Voice Movement Therapy practically and theoretically, I have been driven to research thoroughly the cross-cultural evolution of a therapeutic approach to vocal expression from ancient shamanic practices and spiritual healing to avant garde theatre and present day psychotherapy; and my research has uncovered a rich history of investigation into the healing use of singing and non-verbal vocal expression in many areas and through many ages. This research has enabled me to develop a consolidated body of vocal work which synthesises the practical application of principles drawn from a range of disciplines including psychotherapy, massage, remedial voice training, stress management, singing, music, ethnomusicology and special needs education. The discovery of other previous approaches enabled me to understand what I was doing as the synthesising of fragments emanating from an existing tradition.

Being sceptical of anything which claims to be new and having a deep respect for tradition, I felt determined to ensure that I brought the long-standing practice of a therapeutic approach to vocal expression to the attention of present-day practitioners and students within the relevant professions. I was therefore honoured when Jessica Kingsley invited me to publish a complete and unabridged history of the use of voice and singing in therapy. In this book, *Therapeutic Voicework: Principles and Practice for the Use of Singing as a Therapy* (Newham 1997b), I have described the theoretical and practical history of the subject. In addition, throughout *Therapeutic Voicework* I have related the various historic and extant approaches to vocal expression to the techniques of Voice Movement Therapy. However, the description of the practical techniques which I have evolved are a marginal part of what is primarily a historical and theoretical overview of the field.

In this book, *Using Voice and Song in Therapy: The Practical Application of Voice Movement Therapy*, I speak in a different voice. This book is the second of a series of three volumes which are concerned with the practical application of Voice Movement Therapy. These books are a description of Voice Movement Therapy for those interested in the nitty-gritty of using voice and movement as a therapeutic tool. For it has come to my attention over the past few years that there is an ever increasing interest in the therapeutic value of singing and non-verbal vocal expression amongst therapists from all orientations. Such professionals and students of the therapies are often eager to have an insight into how a therapeutic modality with singing and voice at its centre actually works in practice. In this book and the two other volumes in the series, I shall seek to throw some light on this enquiry and I hope that those seeking to acquaint themselves with an integrated and coherent model of therapeutic vocal work may find inspiration, information and affirmation. Readers interested in the broad historic and theoretical background are referred to my earlier book *Therapeutic Voicework* (Newham 1997b).

Most therapists, teachers and other practitioners working with the hearts and souls of other people recognise that the human voice is a primary medium of communication in human beings. It is an expression of who we are and how we feel. In the timbre of a person's voice you can hear the subtle music of feeling and thought. The ever shifting collage of emotions which we experience infiltrate the voice with tones of happiness, excitement, depression and grief. The human voice is also one way in which we preserve our identity; and the voice and the psychological state of an individual mutually influence each other. The physical condition of the body is also reflected in the vitality of vocal expression: illness, physical debilitation and habitual muscular patterns all take their toll on the way we sound. The voice is an expression of psychological state, a physiological operation and the means by which a person asserts his or her rights within the social order. But many people find themselves negatively affected by psychological dynamics such as stress, anxiety and depression, by physical factors resulting from congenital conditions, illness, injury or bodily misuse and by socially enforced inhibitions. If these effects continue unabated, they often begin to reduce the agility and vitality of body and voice and thereby deplete the capacity for unencumbered expression.

Because the voice is composed of such a complex set of dimensions, the condition of vocal inhibition, restraint or depleted function, from which so many people suffer, leads to an expressive impairment on a psychological, physiological and social level. To reverse the process and revive vocal function therefore necessitates attention to psychological, physical and social processes. Providing these processes are properly understood, working with the voice can be an enlivening way of helping people overcome difficulties which hinder the acoustic and kinetic expression of the Self. And such work may be called Voicework.

Voicework may perhaps best be described as a generic term which includes any work with or on the voice. Within this definition a singing teacher could be said to practise Voicework in developing the vocal skills of her pupils; a bereavement counsellor could be said to practise Voicework in helping a client feel safe and comfortable in giving voice to grief; a speech and language therapist conducts Voicework in helping a patient be relieved of pathological conditions which threaten the health of the voice; a choir leader may be said to practise Voicework in enabling a mass of disparate voices to synthesise into a harmonious whole; a gestalt psychotherapist may draw upon Voicework in assisting a client to give vent to rage through shouts and yells; a répétiteur conducts Voicework when she helps an anxious opera singer with the task of sustaining the demands of the music whilst articulating the poetic text; a music therapist uses Voicework when she helps a young child create a song from a simple rhyme; a priest employs Voicework when using the tonal contours of his voice to communicate to the congregation; a politician uses Voicework when he deliberately employs specific vocal timbres to convince and persuade.

All of these people are using the voice as a channel through which to express or 'push out' something from the inside; and the voice is indeed a major bridge between the inner world of mood, emotion, image, thought and experience and the outer world of relationship, discourse and interaction.

Because the voice is so intimately connected to the expression of feelings and ideas and is a primary channel through which we communicate who we are, Voicework is often innately therapeutic. However, the term Voicework is not synonymous with 'voice therapy'.

The term 'voice therapy' denotes a clinical allopathic field of work conducted by 'voice therapists' who are speech and language therapists with a specialisation in voice disorders. It is also true, however, that a number of medical doctors who have specialised in ear, nose and throat dysfunction and disease (ENT) and who have a special focus on laryngological problems may also call themselves voice therapists. Both ENT doctors and speech therapists alleviate a wide range of disorders and though both kinds of practitioners approach the voice as a somatic phenomenon, increasing numbers of doctors as well as speech and language therapists are beginning to incorporate attendance to the influence of emotional and psychological factors upon the voice.

Although strictly speaking the term 'voice therapy' designates the aforementioned field, in recent years an increasing number of people working in the broad area of 'complementary', 'alternative' or 'holistic' medicine have utilised the term 'voice therapy' to denote the process by which vocalisation through speech, song and non-verbal sound is used as a means through which to express and explore aspects of the psyche. These practitioners utilise the term 'therapy' for its psychic rather than its somatic implication, inviting comparison with the work of psychotherapists rather than speech and language therapists or ENT consultants. However, few of these practitioners are trained in psychotherapy or counselling, which adds further confusion to the vernacular meaning and signification of the term 'voice therapy'. There are also many artistic practitioners, some of long-standing excellence, particularly within the field of the avant garde experimental theatre, who describe their teaching as being, in part, a therapy. This invites the work of theatre practitioners who impart or facilitate vocal work, such as directors, actors and workshop leaders, to be compared to that of a drama therapist. Yet few of these artists are drama therapists. There are also many individuals working in community centres with so-called handicapped children, in mental health wings of hospitals, in special schools and in the voluntary sector who are 'helping' others towards positive change and thus are working therapeutically. Those who utilise vocal expression as part of their approach may understandably be perceived as disseminating 'voice therapy'; yet few of these people have a therapeutic training or qualification.

The widespread use of the term 'therapy' in general and 'voice therapy' specifically is therefore beginning to denote a broad style of work and a particular kind of outcome rather than identifying someone who is trained and qualified in a therapeutic discipline. Furthermore, the word 'therapy', particularly in the current political climate, is subject to so much scrutiny and currently designates such a broad field that it is, for many, time to consider carefully the variety of meanings which the term has.

My assertion is that all approaches to Voicework can most certainly be therapeutic. Moreover, its therapeutic effects can be somatic as well as psychological. This does not, however, necessarily mean that all Voicework practitioners are therapists or that all approaches to Voicework are therapeutic. In fact, many people have suffered the most abominable anti-therapeutic treatment in the hands of voice coaches, singing teachers and voice workshop leaders who, whilst artistically and technically competent in the field of voice, have not the slightest insight into the foundations of compassion and analysis upon which a truly therapeutic contract is built.

Voice Movement Therapy may be described as a particular approach to Voicework and a specifically crafted form of therapeutic Voicework. Voice Movement Therapy can help people whose expressive activity has been detrimentally influenced by emotional problems, trauma and mental illness, those whose lives have been turned around by the effects of severe injury or the development of diseases such as Multiple Sclerosis, those with congenital conditions such as cerebral palsy and Down's Syndrome and those who have been discouraged from asserting or expressing themselves by overpowering and infertile environmental influences. In addition, Voice Movement Therapy can respond to the needs of those whose social or professional predicament places exceptional demands upon the voice, who often find themselves ill equipped to preserve the health and longevity of their vocal instrument and therefore require education and rehabilitation. No less important are those who, whilst healthy and not overtly impeded, can nonetheless discover an increased potential for expression and creativity through singing and sound-making.

If not conducted with skill and expertise, however, Voice Movement Therapy can also be threatening to the health of mind and body; and there are some people for whom any kind of therapeutic Voicework, including Voice Movement Therapy, may not be expedient for the maintenance of health, no matter how proficient the practitioner. As a consequence, someone practising any kind of Voicework needs to be competent in understanding the psychophysical nature of vocal expression; and in addition they must learn to recognise those for whom Voicework is an inappropriate medium through which to work for physical or psychological reasons.

In my view, though there are many resourceful, sensitive and proficient voice practitioners administering many diverse approaches to Voicework, some therapeutic and some not, nonetheless any Voicework practitioner, particularly a practitioner working with an overt therapeutic dimension, should be trained to do so.

All students of the professional training in Voice Movement Therapy undergo a thorough physical and psychological journey in order to facilitate the same in others. In addition, all trainees study creative, allopathic and psychological models of intervention and analysis. They are thereby trained to be practitioners who can deal effectively with the psychological and physical aspects of vocal expression and who, in suspecting serious pathology of mind or body, will refer the client to an appropriate practitioner.

Voice Movement Therapy can be conducted with individuals and with groups. The clients begin by making their most effortless natural sound whilst the acoustic tones of the voice and the muscle tone of the body are heard and observed. In response to an informed analysis of breathing, sound and movement the practitioner massages and manipulates the client's body, gives instruction in ways of moving and suggests moods and images which the client allows to affect and infiltrate the vocal timbre. The voice is thereby sculptured and animated through a graphic and authentic expression of the Self. In order to facilitate this process, the practitioner also offers pedagogic technical training by which the voice develops in range and malleability; this helps the client find access to sounds which give expression to hitherto dormant aspects of the Self. The result of such Voicework is psychologically uplifting, physically invigorating, creatively rejuvenating and serves to release vocal function from constriction.

As the process unfolds, the client is encouraged and enabled to use creative writing from which lyrics for songs are drawn. The practitioner then helps the client create songs which are vocalised using the broadest possible range of the voice, giving artistic expression to personal material. In addition, the spectrum of voices which are elicited during the process are used as the basis from which to create characters which symbolise and express different aspects of the Self. Voice Movement Therapy thereby draws on dance, music and drama and in many ways, therefore, provides a model for an integrated expressive arts therapy where creative movement, creative writing, music and theatre are synthesised into a coherent strategy within which all strands are linked by the common thread of the voice. However, Voice Movement Therapy differs from other arts therapies in that it necessarily appropriates a physiological dimension, as the voice is so often the locus for somatic and psychosomatic difficulties – and a complete understanding of vocal expression is not possible without an appreciation of the way the voice functions physiologically.

The techniques which constitute Voice Movement Therapy can, therefore, be loosely divided into three areas. The first of these areas is the use of voice with movement, dance and massage and is covered in the first volume of this series: *Using Voice and Movement in Therapy*. The second area is the use of voice with creative writing and singing, which is covered in this volume: *Using Voice and Song in Therapy*. The third area is the use of voice with drama and performance, which is covered in the third volume: *Using Voice and Theatre in Therapy*.

These books aim to be both theoretically informative and practically inspiring. For, though the use of Voice Movement Therapy as a mode of therapeutic inquiry, like all disciplines, requires training, there are parts of the Voice Movement Therapy methodology which therapists from other orientations can borrow from, adapt and utilise. I hope that the techniques described in this book will inspire practitioners to broaden their field of enquiry to include vocal expression.

Naturally, the untrained, unconsidered use of vocal expression in a therapeutic context is potentially dangerous; and many of the techniques which constitute Voice Movement Therapy require practical training to know how to administer them. This is not a handbook. At the end of the day, each reader must employ a discernment in keeping with the brevity of the subject's treatment here.

Throughout the book I not only give case studies but also reprint clients' own accounts of their experience of the work; and I am grateful to those who have permitted me to tell their story and quote their words. Nonetheless, names and other details have been altered to preserve confidentiality and anonymity.

CHAPTER I

Tales, Myths and Legends
The Archetypal Context of Voice and Psyche

On Therapy, Loss and Refinding Your Self

Most people come into therapy because they have lost a part of their soul, their psyche, their Self. Some people have lost their joy, others have lost a loved one, a relationship or a marriage; some have lost their trust and sense of safety due to a traumatic experience, others have lost their self-confidence and belief in themselves; some people have lost their sexuality and their vitality; others have lost their aggression and ability to assert themselves. One of the most common losses which people come into therapy to retrieve is the loss of voice.

Therapy is not only concerned with the content of what is voiced – it is also focused on the act of giving voice itself. Therapy takes place inside an acoustic vessel where the unconscious resounds and is echoed through crescendos and tempos to which the practitioner must be acutely sensitive. The act of giving voice contains the healing balm; vocalising is self-empowerment in its most rudimentary and most primal manifestation. When we give voice to parts of the Self which have remained mute hitherto, then we reclaim, refind and rediscover something that had been lost.

In order for this therapeutic process to occur, the client must first find the voice with which to resound the lost parts of the Self. Initially, therapy is about finding a voice.

The loss of voice is a universal contemporary psychological problem. For many people, the process of becoming an adult is a process of becoming increasingly silenced. And therapy is a process of reversing this detrimental developmental act of making mute the spontaneous expression of the Self.

The fact that the loss of an authentic voice is such a widespread phenomenon is reflected in the proliferate occurrence of the voice as a motif in myths, legends and fairy tales throughout European culture. When clients come into therapy to work on their voice, they bring with them not only the personal and idiosyncratic details of their particular silences and inhibitions. They also walk an archetypal path, living out aspects of patterns which testify to problems inherent in the human condition. It is therefore useful to begin by examining a few of the most widely known tales which deal with the psychology of voice and its shadow called silence.

Orpheus in the Underworld

The relationship between voice and loss is encapsulated powerfully in the story of the Greek hero Orpheus, who is the classical symbol of song as well as representing the inevitability of human loss. Orpheus was born to the God Apollo and his lover Calliope and from the moment he was born he sang out with a golden voice that amazed everyone. When it was time for Orpheus to leave home, his father gave him a stringed instrument called a lyre so that Orpheus could accompany his beautiful singing.

One afternoon, whilst Orpheus was passing through a forest, he noticed a beautiful woman dancing and fell in love with her at first sight. This woman's name was Eurydice. But, at the height of their delicious love affair on a hot sunny day, Orpheus fell asleep in a lemon grove whilst Eurydice was picking berries. It was here that according to some she was raped and according to others she was poisoned by a serpent. Whichever is true, she was taken to the underworld, the land of the dead ruled by a relentless figure called Hades.

When Orpheus discovered the fate of his beloved he despaired, because he knew that no one living could enter the underworld and once there, no one could return. Yet, he thought of his voice and its powers. He reflected upon how he had used his voice to calm aggressors, to assuage storms, to seduce lovers and to talk to the beasts. Perhaps, thought Orpheus, his voice would be powerful enough to guide him into the underworld and rescue his dear Eurydice.

Fearless and determined, Orpheus followed his lover's footsteps down through the face of the earth and into the underworld. He met Charon the Ferryman whom he had to persuade to transport him across the river Styx; he met Cerberus the three-headed hound of Hades; and he encountered hellish characters and terrifying monsters. But, each time he met a new obstacle he drew upon his voice and sang with such power and such heart that his aggressors cleared the path and pointed him to his destination.

When Orpheus reached the centre of the underworld he came face to face with Hades and pleaded with him to let Eurydice return to the light of the living world with him. Hades was so struck by the urgency of Orpheus' love and so moved by the spirit of Orpheus' voice that he agreed to let him take Eurydice with him – on one condition. Orpheus was not to turn back to look at Eurydice until they were both back upon the earth.

Wasting no time, Orpheus proceeded back the way he had come, with Eurydice following closely behind him. They travelled again through gorge and crag, across the river Styx and back up towards the earth's floor. But, with only a short distance left to travel, Orpheus could no longer resist and he turned to gaze upon his lover. In this moment Eurydice was snatched by the winds of the underworld and Orpheus lost her forever. So grief-stricken was Orpheus that he cried and cried and cried and his cries led to songs which echoed throughout the lands for an eternity.

The Foolishness of Looking

It is natural to wonder why Orpheus turned to look at Eurydice; for surely he would have heard her footsteps behind him. We can only imagine that Orpheus did not trust his ears as much as his eyes. And, if not, why did he not use his precious voice to call to her? The voice had not been prohibited; the gaze had. Had he given voice, perhaps she would have resounded in response and Orpheus might have heard the presence of her soul. But instead he turned to look upon her. The soul cannot be seen, it is not visible and cannot be located, dissected, placed under the microscope and observed. The soul will not subject itself to an autopsy, which means to see automatically with the eye. The soul evades the eye; and the more we attempt to look at the soul the more it escapes our understanding and our grasp. Though light enlightens it also burns; and the delicacy of the soul's fabric must be protected from the scorching rays of the inquisitive lamp. This was the lesson that Orpheus learned. Eurydice was in his trail; yet he could not trust the sound of her footsteps. He had to turn to look, to gaze, to see. And, caught by the terrifying light of his gaze, the poor soul was taken forever.

If we want to solicit the company of the soul then we must refrain from placing it under the light of our gaze. We must stave off our optical fascinations and learn to listen to the soul instead. For though the soul is invisible it is not inaudible. We can perceive the soul with our ears. In fact the word 'audience' does not mean those who see but those who hear.

Because the soul is invisible and makes itself known through sound, we have to trust our own ears if we are to hear the language of the soul. And the language of the soul to which our ears must be open is the language of the human voice. This instrument with which most of us are blessed is, as

Orpheus discovered, capable of calming and placating monsters. And of course the monsters by which we are most threatened are the monsters in our own selves: the monsters we call depression and anxiety, the monsters we call guilt and shame, the monsters we call shyness and loneliness, the monsters which inhibit and enrage us; and the monsters which we call loss and grief which were the most daunting of the monsters which Orpheus finally overcame through singing. All of the negative forces and influences to which we are prey are like the monsters which Orpheus met on his journey. And just as Orpheus calmed the monsters in his path with song, so too we can calm our own inner monsters through singing. Singing disperses fear and bandages our wounds. Singing lifts our spirits and settles our nerves. Singing discharges our emotions and animates the heart. Singing gives shape to a soul that cannot be seen.

The Echoes of Therapy

On the surface of the story, Eurydice is Orpheus' lover. But psychologically she is more than this, for she represents a part of his soul that is lost and must be reclaimed.

Most people come into therapy in response to a recognition that something has been lost. Therapy represents Psyche's lamp and holds the promise that her shining light will lead us to the spot where we lost that which we seek. Therapy will help us refind those parts of our Self of which we have been robbed by the passage of time.

Among the common losses which bring people to therapy is the loss of voice and many people come into therapy because they seek to refind their voice. In fact, traditionally, therapy is all about giving voice. The therapeutic process which Freud initiated provided a vessel in which the patient's voice could be echoed, amplified and heard; and therapeutic process has remained an essentially acoustic process ever since. But it had not always been like this. With Freud, therapy moves from a voyeuristic observation of silent victims to an active listening to the tales of those who have been silenced. Prior to Freud, therapy had been an optical rather than an acoustic concern, typified most acutely by the work of Freud's predecessor Jean Martin Charcot.

Jean Martin Charcot worked in the Salpêtrière Clinic in Paris where his studies in hysteria began in 1870 and where he was the first theorist to see hysteria as psychological rather than physiological in origin. He also showed that hysteria was suffered by men and therefore not limited solely to women. Charcot frequently presented his female hysterics to audiences in public lecture theatres, encouraging them to perform *attitudes passionelles*: a physical and theatrical mime show which replayed their lives and emotions. As a result, several patients became stars or celebrities of his 'hysteria shows', later becoming immortalised in the collection of photographed gestures and hysterical expressions called *Iconographique de la Salpêtrière*.

While we have a full pictorial record of Charcot's hysterical patients, only a few fragments of their words were recorded. However, in 1895 Freud and Breuer published the results of their analyses of so-called hysterical women under the title *Studies in Hysteria*. Here, for the first time, the patient's own voices were taken seriously and the words which they uttered were written down. Their stories, memories, dreams, and fantasies thus entered the medical record and psychoanalysis was founded upon intimate conversations between hysterical women and male psychiatrists. Therapy had moved from picture to voice, from optical exhibitions to verbal dialogues. Freud's case studies marked an important departure in psychological analysis, from the pictorial emphasis in the work of Freud's predecessor and teacher Charcot, to the auditory skills of listening and attending to women's stories and voices. In many ways, Freud gave women a voice, or rather he listened to their voices, which only makes the process by which he allegedly distorted and misrepresented them more tragic.

Despite Freud's later distractions which served to distort and sabotage the very voices which he had elicited, the original idea of psychoanalysis was to give the suffering a voice. It so happened that most of those who seemed to be suffering were women; and the political implications of Freud's initial project was to give those women who had been muted by circumstance a voice which could be released without restraint in the confidential chambers of the consulting room.

Today, most political analyses of these troubled women agree that their problems stemmed in large part from the stifling and repressive patriarchy which enveloped the nineteenth century and continued to stifle women through the majority of the twentieth century. Women's voices were subservient to men's voices. In fact, a woman's voice was considered to be best employed as a reflection and reverberation of a man's voice. Women had no platform of their own.

It remains true today that our voice is influenced by the nature of those who hear it. We live in relationship and our primary relationships provide an acoustic vessel which reverberates, dampens, heightens or stifles our voice.

In therapy, one of the most common problems which people bring is the feeling that their most intimate and primary relationship does not provide sufficient room for their voice to be heard. And many people, particularly women, report that they have no voice of their own but act merely as a reflection of their partner's sonic self. Such a situation is represented perfectly in the myth of Echo and Narcissus.

Echo and Narcissus

In Greek mythology Echo was a mountain nymph who assisted Zeus, supreme ruler of mortals and gods, in having yet another secret love affair by keeping his wife Hera distracted with idle chatter whilst he was away. So with the incessant and interminable contours of her voice, Echo engaged Hera in an infinite rapport about everything and nothing. However, when Hera discovered how she had been deceived, she punished Echo by making her unable to speak except to repeat the last words of someone else she heard. So it was that the speaking voice of Echo, which had been her spell, her talent and her proclivity became her handicap and her foible. Then, to make matters worse, she fell foolishly in love with Narcissus.

Narcissus was a beautiful youth who refused love from the many hundreds of nymphs who fell at his feet, including Echo; for Narcissus could love no one. Then, one day Narcissus caught the sight of his face mirrored in a pool of water and fell in love with his own reflection. Unable to grasp what he saw, Narcissus pined away and died for love of himself. In the aftermath of his death Echo wilted and withered away in mourning of the love she never had until all that remained of her was her voice.

Echo and Narcissus make a fatal and cataclysmic pair which epitomises many unfortunate relationships: a man in love with his own reflection and a woman who can do nothing but reflect the voice of the man she loves. As his identity thrives and excels so she loses all sense of Self other than to act as his servile supporter and abettor.

Narcissus and Echo are in many ways opposites. He is alive with his own confidence to the point of an overbearing self-indulgence which precludes him from loving anyone but himself. She is so transfixed and revering of another in her desperate attempt to be loved that she has no original words to utter and no voice that is truly her own. It is, in my experience, often the woman in a relationship or marriage that struggles the hardest to keep her voice alive. Indeed, many women seem to pay the price of their voice in return for the man they love, playing into the web of misogyny that prefers a woman to be modest of tongue. Such a sacrifice is immortalised in the fairy tale 'The Little Mermaid'.

The Little Mermaid

The Little Mermaid was the youngest of six mermaids who lived with their father at the bottom of the ocean. As children they were not permitted to go up to the surface of the waves; but on their fifteenth birthday they were free to swim wherever they pleased. So when it came to the Little Mermaid's fifteenth year she travelled upwards, swam to a ship and peered in through one of the portholes where she saw a beautiful Prince with whom she fell in love at first sight. But then a storm grew and tossed the ship from side to side, tearing down its masts and wrecking its bough. The whole crew were thrown into the ocean and the Prince choked and spat and passed into a deep sleep. So the Little Mermaid carried the Prince to the shore and then swam back out to sea where she watched until a beautiful young woman came, awoke the prince and took him to safety.

The Little Mermaid returned to the bottom of the ocean but spent her days in mourning, longing to be rid of her fish's tail and to have two legs so she might enter the world of the land and win the love of the Prince whom she had saved from death but who had never set eyes on her.

So, the Little Mermaid went to the Sea Witch who said: 'I know what you want. It is stupid of you, but you shall have your way, for it will bring you grief, my pretty Princess. You want to get rid of your fish-tail and to have two legs instead, like those the people of the earth walk with, so that the young Prince might fall in love with you. Very well, I will prepare a potion for you; and when you drink it your tail will shrivel up and become legs. But it will hurt you. It will seem as if you have been cut with a sharp sword. You will have a graceful walk and no dancer will be able to move as lightly as you. But every step you take will be as if you have trodden upon sharp knives. If you can bear this, I can help you.'

'Yes!' said the Little Mermaid, 'Please give me the potion.'

'But you must pay me for my costly potion,' said the witch. 'You have the finest voice of all the mermaids; and it is with your voice that you intend to enchant your fair Prince. But this voice you must give to me as payment for my potion.'

'But if you take away my voice,' said the Little Mermaid, 'what will remain?'

'Your beautiful form, your graceful walk and your speaking eyes,' said the witch, 'with those you can capture a man's heart.'

The Little Mermaid looked afraid, as the witch asked her if she had lost her courage. 'No, I have not lost my courage,' replied the Little Mermaid.

'Very well then,' said the witch, 'put out your little tongue so that I may cut it off for my payment.' And indeed the Little Mermaid put out her tongue and the Sea Witch sheared it clean off so that now the Little Mermaid was mute. As if this were not enough, the Little Mermaid had to agree that if she failed to win the love of her Prince she would immediately give up her life, be thrown into the sea and be turned to foam.

When the Little Mermaid drank the potion it felt as if a sword were splitting her into two pieces and she fell into a deep sleep. But when she awoke she saw the Prince standing before her and noticed that her fish-tail had gone and that in its place were two legs crowned with sweet white feet. The Prince led the silent beauty to his castle where they danced, every step biting her feet with a searing pain and in time the Prince became very fond of this silent girl but never thought to make her his wife. For he was to marry the woman who had discovered him upon the shore.

When the marriage day arrived, the Little Mermaid knew that she would die that night, for she had failed to win the Prince's love. But, as she stood by the shore soothing her burning feet in the ocean, her five sisters appeared. 'We have hacked off our hair and given it to the Sea Witch in payment for your life to be spared,' spoke the oldest sister. 'Here is a knife sent by the witch. Tonight you must plunge the knife into the Prince's heart and as he falls to his death, the blood that falls onto your feet will cause your fish-tail to grow again and you may return to the sea as a mermaid once more.'

But when the night came, the Little Mermaid could not do the deed and instead hurled the knife into the ocean. With this defiance she gave up her life and was thrown into the sea where she melted into foam.

There are women in every city of every country to this day who reach the verge of killing their husbands to save themselves from life-threatening abuse. Few women respond to this urge; instead they stay mute and sacrifice themselves to their ordeal. For such women, giving up their voice in the hope of peace, as the Little Mermaid gave her tongue to the Sea Witch in return for the promise of love, is not enough. They must give up their lives and suffer the agony of walking on sharp knives, following in the agonising footsteps of the Little Mermaid.

The girl who is made to silently endure terrible pains in total muteness is a common motif in many fairy tales and is portrayed particularly vividly in the three stories: 'The Twelve Brothers' and the 'Six Swans', recorded by the Grimm Brothers and 'The Wild Swans' recorded by Hans Christian Anderson. In these tales a girl is born and all of her brothers either die or are turned into birds. When the girl realises that her birth has caused the horror of her brothers' fate she agrees to all kinds of ordeals in order to restore them to life and human shape. In all of these tales, in addition to completing tasks set by a sadistic power-monger, the girl must remain mute, refrain from laughing, weeping, singing or speaking a single word until her tasks are complete. Eventually, she is saved by a prince who marries her in spite of her silence; or perhaps because he prefers it.

In many fairy tales, female virtue is associated with verbal modesty and restraint and a fair Princess is always softly spoken when she is not silent. Masculine virtue, meanwhile, is associated with an outspoken tongue and the courage to speak up and speak out.

Many women and men come into therapy in an attempt to rewrite the fairytale of the muted soul and reclaim the power of their voice. In archetypal terms, this therapeutic endeavour is directed towards rediscovering the siren – a psychic component which is essential to psychological survival.

The Song of the Siren

Bluebeard, a character in a tale written by Perrault in 1697, is like the prototype for all the deranged serial killers and women haters of present-day cinematic imagination. He lives in a grand castle where he houses a succession of wives. To each wife he gives a key which opens a door to a room which he forbids her to open and forbids her to enter. She must hold the key but refrain from acting upon her curiosity. But each wife is unable to resist and enters the forbidden chamber where she discovers the dead bodies of the previous wives hanging by a noose on a rail. Each wife's punishment for disobeying the master and using the key to unlock the morbid entrance is to join the bodies of all her predecessors upon the rack of ropes. But, the last wife has a sister called Anne whose voice is as loud and as piercing as a siren and she manages to call for help from the cliff top as Bluebeard is about to murder his next bride. Recognising the voice of their sister, Anne's brothers gallop to the rescue and put an end to Bluebeard's scheme.

Anne's voice is a siren. It warns of danger and it attracts the heroes to the scene of the crime. Without Anne's voice, her sister would have met the fate of all the previous brides at Bluebeard's wicked hands.

In 1819, a Frenchman called Cagniard de la Tour invented an instrument which emitted extremely high sounds. He named this instrument a *siréne*. Fifty years later his invention was adapted to create foghorns for ships. Cagniard de la Tour unwittingly bequeathed the word 'siren' to common usage and this word is still used to describe machines which give warning of the presence of danger through their unceasing voice.

In Greek mythology the Sirens were sea nymphs with wings and claws and the body of a bird whilst the Sirens' faces were human and as beautiful as any woman. But the Sirens' most astounding feature was the exquisite beauty and tremendous power of their voices which would charm and allure any who heard the Sirens sing. The Sirens lived on the rocky shores of the ocean. But unlike the foghorn adapted from Cagniard de la Tour's siren which stood upon the cliffs and steered the ships away from collision, the Sirens lured the sailors towards them until they were irresistibly impelled to cast themselves into the sea to their destruction.

When Odysseus consulted Circe for sound advice before setting sail on one of his many voyages, she told him that he and his seamen should stop up their ears with bees wax before sailing past the Sirens' island so that they would not be lured by the Sirens' sweet song. She advised Odysseus to have his men bind him to the mast before sailing past the shores of the Sirens' habitat and told him to instruct his crew not to release him until well clear of the Sirens' seductive call.

As the crew sailed passed the Sirens' land, Odysseus could hear the ravishing melodies of their song. The Sirens' serenade was prophetic and promised Odysseus foreknowledge of all things that would come to pass on earth if he ventured into their company. Tempted by the Sirens' promise of knowledge and foresight Odysseus struggled to tear himself free from the mast; but his crew were faithful to his previous instructions and bound him faster to the wood. As they sailed, the music grew fainter until they were once again in the clear silent swoon of the sea, whereupon Odysseus was released from his bondage and the entire crew unsealed their ears. The Sirens were so vexed at failing to lure Odysseus that they threw themselves into the suicidal drink of the ocean where their voices were interminably drowned.

A Siren is a temptress, a seductress. But she tempts and seduces with the promise of knowledge and foresight; and her voice is the carrier and emissary of all that she knows. The Sirens are named according to their voices: Aglaophonos, which means Lovely Voice; Ligeia, which means Shrill; Molpe, which means Music; and Thelxepeia, which means Spellbinding Words. The Siren's voice is one that enchants and beckons and their hungry call lures their prey. Men are both enraptured and terrified of the Sirens' voice because it sings of things beyond the domain of their rationale.

In early times, the Sirens could fly and if passing sailors did not respond to their call they would attack the ships from the air. In later times, stories were told of how the Muses stole their wing tips and left them earthbound and seabound. As tales of the Sirens passed from lip to tongue through the retelling of their lure across the centuries they lost their claws as well as their wings and began to live not upon the rocky shores but deep below the current at the bottom of the ocean. In time, the Sirens became mermaids with the upper body and radiant face of womanly beauty and a fishes tail. But the mermaids retained the magnificent voice bequeathed by the Sirens of old.

Reclaiming the Voice

Originally, fairy tales were invented and told by women in the parlours of seventeenth-century Europe. Fairy tales were, before the printing press and the dissemination of the written tale, a powerful form of feminine expression. They were told and retold, adapted and changed to contain the codes and messages which communicated the essence of the human condition as seen from the female tale-teller's perspective. With the proliferation of the written word, men took over the role of recording the tales and they became fixed in the ink-dried symbol of patriarchal power: the printed word.

The power of the original tales was that they bridged the gap between highly personal experience and narratives which had a universal relevance. The inventors of fairy tales would take an event or a story from personal experience and amplify it, turning real people into inflated caricatures. In many ways, the tale-tellers were creating a therapy rooted in archetypal psychology. From an array of personal experiences, the tale-tellers would find a thread of themes and motifs which resonated with the listeners and weave a web which made a personal story relevant and psychologically meaningful to all those present.

The therapeutic power of creating a fairy tale from the realms of personal experience is as useful and liberating now as it was in the seventeenth century. It gives men and women an opportunity to rifle and rummage amongst the images of their history and create from it an artful narrative which transforms the burden of individual experience into the elevation of communion.

One of the problems with Freud's original vision was that it assumed that healing could arise from the repetition of one's own personal recollections. Today, many people come into an expressive arts therapy because verbal psychotherapy has failed to provide the transformative leap from a repetitious telling of their story to the creation of a fresh narrative within which to live in the present.

Therapy begins with creation of the new. Yet, at the same time, experience is written indelibly upon the psyche. Our story is a neurological calligraphy. The art of creating story, tale and illusion is that it accepts the indelible calligraphy of personal experience whilst at the same time moving it onto the plane of shared identity. In Voice Movement Therapy, one of the therapeutic processes which I have seen yield positive results in many people involves the client in the art of retelling their biography and turning this into fairy tale and, eventually, song.

CHAPTER 2

From Biography to Fairy Tale
Creating Therapeutic Communion
with the Art of Telling

Past, Present and Future

Therapy is chronological; it exists in time. Indeed, time is present everywhere in therapy. Time holds the session between its beginning and its end. Time measures the process of change, provides a barometer and set of co-ordinates. Time heals, frustrates and agitates. Time remains permanent in a sea of psychic transitions. Time comes and goes. Time tells that the session has begun and then, just as we forget its looming presence, time is up and our healing hour is over for another day or another week.

When a new client comes into therapy the most dominating aspect of time is the echo of times past. The client enters therapy at a junction, realising that their present time is shaped by the past and that the past must be repositioned in relation to the present if the future is to hold a promise of good times to come. The client talks of the past, bringing into the present time of the session stories from early childhood, tales from a year or so ago and things which happened only last month or maybe even yesterday. This past is unfolded like the canvas of a habitat which the client will inhabit for the duration of therapy. The therapist meanwhile listens and remembers.

In the early time of therapy, much of what the client discloses is a case history of body and mind: surgical procedures, major illnesses, periods of mental anguish, periods of medication, name of doctor, medical history of the family. This gives the therapist a sense of the facts of time: the way that time has treated the client and the scars which its ticking hands have left upon the psyche and soma.

Sequence is often important in this unfolding. The therapist's keen ears listen for the way times of physical illness are coincident with events in the social and familial fabric of the client's past. Things which seem disconnected often radiate a numinous relationship; and connections previously made by the client appear insubstantial and irrelevant.

When the tales of times past are woven and the fabric of its myth is hung, the client begins to speak of present time: his joys and loathings, his needs and frustrations, his worries and proclivities. Again, the therapist listens and remembers. Then, the time of future rears its head as the client begins to muse of the horizon and braves to ask time for the future fruits of possibility.

The therapist and client now engage in a dialogue of time, seeking out the calligraphy, the intersections and the lines of stress which connect past, present and future.

These words of the client's telling may or may not be written down. Some therapists keep copious notes; others store information in the private corridors of their mind. But whether scored on paper or brain, a story has been told and part of the therapeutic potential of the story is contained within its artistic value as oral and literary art. The person who should write it down is the client.

The Therapeutic Art of Autobiography

Many people, particularly those whose lives have been riddled with more than a fair share of suffering, speak idly in cafes and bars about writing a book of their life. When people begin thinking about their life they sense its magnitude and ominous audacity, and they muse about writing it all down one day. Few of these people would consider therapy; many of them may not even have a clear sense of what psychotherapy is. Yet their reasons for contemplating writing are therapeutic, as though the act of creating an artful story from the remnants of one's own journey has the power to raise up a sense of good even from the bad times.

Those people who do come into therapy tend to speak of their story, giving acoustic shape to their tale in the resonating vessel of the consulting room. Those who choose an artistic form of therapy, such as drama therapy or music therapy, after some years of verbal psychotherapy, may be tired of telling and retelling the tales of their woes and may welcome an opportunity to work through a non-verbal therapeutic discipline, escaping the pressure to trace their footsteps once again.

But telling the story impromptu to the diagnostic ears of a clinician is not the same as artfully sculpturing a tale upon the page. The former is a clinical necessity, the latter is an artistic choice.

When we write our story in the form of an autobiography, what was once entirely personal becomes communicative and to some degree collective. For we listen to ourselves write upon the page as if through the ears of a reader. We create a sense of destiny, of self-control, of editorial choice. Though we cannot rewrite the events of our history we can reposition them upon the page, bringing the landscape of our memory into relief with new-found focus.

Many people come into therapy to rewrite their life, to construct a new script, a new prose and a new poesis. This is a mammoth task. It is a violent task. And it is a creative task. Writing of oneself involves scoring upon the page lines of events linked by time which mirror the memories of events which are scored upon the psyche. The pen gouges, burrows, digs and unearths. The pen is mightier than the sword; but like the sword it separates one thing from another. Writing helps us sort out the pieces, the images, the characters and the years. And from this writing something new is formed: an artifact, a template, a canvas, a literary event. And this event marks the beginning of a new time.

Practical Method: The Autobiography

In Voice Movement Therapy, during the early stages of the therapeutic process, the client is asked to write their autobiography. Beginning with first memories and tracing their childhood through to adulthood, the client creates a written text including descriptions of their family and friends as well as major events which they feel have shaped their lives.

To help the client focus it is useful to suggest that they set aside specific writing periods – usually an hour per day for one or two weeks. The client may use the first set of writing hours to draft the story and the latter periods to rewrite and make the editorial alterations and adjustments which bring the autobiography to fruition.

When the task is completed, the next stage offers the client an opportunity to read the autobiography aloud – to the practitioner in individual work and to the entire ensemble in group work. The audience is asked to listen generously and not to intervene or remark in any way.

The following are excerpts from the autobiographies of two clients from a Voice Movement Therapy group. The first is by Vicky, who came into therapy to deal with the consequences of having been repeatedly orally sexually abused by her father. The second is by Richard, who came into therapy to deal with the consequences of having survived an aeroplane accident in which most other passengers died.

Client's Autobiography: Vicky

The Girl with No Arms

...My father always held my arms down and I remember them going numb and hurting. Physically it was the most painful part of the ordeal. He usually held them down with his knees, sitting on top of me, but sometimes he would clasp them with his huge hands...

He used to put his prick in my mouth and tell me to suck gently and slowly. Then he would climax and my mouth would fill up with sperm. I remember that the pain in my arms was so great that I wanted him to have an orgasm so he would release my arms. When he did I could feel the muscles in my arms tingling and it would take a while for the feeling to return to them...

After my father had left the room I would lie there for a while and then spit the sperm out into some tissues. But most of it would be swallowed. I didn't want to swallow it but it just happened so that by the time I was able to get up after he had left the room it was all in my throat...

I still have trouble with my arms today. I can't do anything for very long like writing or drawing or anything that involves the use of my arm muscles. And my throat still feels all clogged up.

Client's Autobiography: Richard

Getting the Feet on the Ground

I was raised to believe in myself but to have humility and grace also. My parents were both Quakers but were also extremely successful business people. We were very wealthy and all my brothers and sisters have also made a great success of their careers.

According to my mother, of all her children I was the one with the loudest voice. I was very outspoken and many of my teachers apparently found me difficult to deal with. As an adult I continued to have a loud voice, both literally and metaphorically. I had no trouble making myself heard and in my work a lot of weight rested upon my decisions...

It was a trip that I had no enthusiasm for and, in fact, I had considered cancelling it...

When we were all boarded, the pilot mentioned that the weather was bad and that we should expect some turbulence. I did not think much of it and continued to read my newspaper.

But then, disaster struck and mayhem broke out. The whole plane was torn apart and people were screaming and yelling. The most awful thing was that the person sitting next to me was decapitated. I cannot describe in words the terror...

As a result of the accident my entire life changed. My wife divorced me, I lost my job, I became an insomniac and, most markedly, my voice disappeared.

The accident left me shy and nervous and the actual quality of my voice completely changed. It became soft and timid and reticent. I no longer recognised the sound of my own voice. Metaphorically, I also lost my voice in the world. I no longer had any confidence in my opinions and had no capacity to tell others what to do.

Before the accident my one hobby had been to sing in a choir. This was no longer possible. I could not sing a note.

The Ancient Story Circle

Often, during the reading of the autobiography, the client will express emotions provoked by particular chapters in the story. Stoic clients who tell their story with a dry detachment during therapy will, in response to reading their own writing, often weep as they speak. Also, the group of listeners will often be moved to experience a tender and vulnerable disposition as they empathise with the story told.

The exercise of rewriting and reading the autobiography is not only pertinent and appropriate to individual therapy; it is also a rich and enlightening process that can be conducted with many kinds of groups whose purposes may be recreational, educational or therapeutic. The process of sitting in a circle, reading your own story and listening to the stories of others acts as a kind of initiation for the members of a group who are meeting one another for the first time and who are about to embark upon a journey of discovery.

This therapeutic process is rooted in an age-old tradition of a story circle where people gather and share tales of woe and joy, victory and repression. In the moment of telling, the empathy of the audience rescues the teller from isolation. For empathy cannot be engendered unless the empathisers can genuinely relate to the story told from their own experience. As soon as this occurs, the teller is no longer alone and the problems of the teller become those of the listeners. Audience and performer become one in an act of psychic participation. This returns therapy to the origin of catharsis. For Aristotle's observations of the psychodynamics of Greek theatre from which Freud extrapolated a cathartic therapy were that the audience experienced a therapeutic catharsis as a result of their empathy with the story. The catharsis and the healing were engendered in the audience not in the performers. In true cathartic tradition, very often, the therapeutic catharsis in Voice Movement Therapy is experienced by those who listen to the tale told by a teller as much as by the teller herself. However, the effect of the listening group's empathy in turn deepens the healing effect for the teller. It is not the telling itself but the quality of listening which creates an acoustic therapeutic vessel for the client.

Client's Account: Vicky

Though I had told the story of my childhood sexual abuse many times in therapy – in fact with three different psychotherapists – the act of writing it as an autobiography and then reading it to an audience of others who were present with their own stories was a completely different experience.

I felt strangely separate from my story, yet at the same time completely inside it. The word that comes to mind is 'solidarity'. I felt a solidarity with the people I was reading to. I think this came from realising that I was not describing the events to an analytic therapist. I was reading my story to a group of people who were like me. I felt they were resonating with me. At times I would look up and notice others in the group crying in response to my story. Though I felt a little guilty at causing tears, at the same time I felt healed by the presence of this genuine emotion. The group seemed to be saying: 'Yes, I hear this story and I share these feelings'. Though it sounds odd, I felt loved and held.

Having a story to tell that was written on the page gave me a sense of limits. Usually, when I talk about myself, I feel like I go on and on incessantly and I never know how to finish or when to finish – as though I am looking for the right words as I speak and they never come. But having a story to tell where I had already been through the process of editing and arranging helped me deliver what I wanted to say which felt direct. I felt like I was being heard because I was getting through. I was communicating.

Client's Account: Richard

For me, the act of choosing what to write and then hearing myself read the chosen words aloud to the group felt like an incredible step forward. Part of my suffering since the accident has been a terrible lack of confidence in making any decisions and this was reflected in my difficulty in deciding what words to put upon the page. When I had written my autobiography, I felt a great sense of achievement. But also, because I started from when I was very young and wrote up to the present, I was able to make connections between the accident and my previous life story. I discovered a kind of logic.

When we came to read excerpts from the autobiography I was terrified because I thought I would open my mouth and nothing would come out. But having the script of the written words was very useful. I heard myself read as though listening to a stranger. For the first time, I felt a small space, a small distance between me and my troubles. Nonetheless, I still hated the sound of my voice which sounded like a shell of my former self.

The Therapeutic Art of the Fairy Tale

Fairy tales provide a sharp and powerful allegory for psychological experience and have been used in proliferation within therapy to help clients understand their sufferings as more than entirely personal. When a client recognises their story in the predicament of a fairy tale character, they see that what they are going through is in some ways part of a universal necessity and inevitability.

Usually, when fairy tales are used in therapy, they are employed interpretatively by the therapist who draws parallels between the psychic activity within the client and the narrative and imagistic activity within the tale. But clients can be empowered greatly by transforming their own autobiographies into an original fairy tale where fathers become kings, sisters become princesses, houses become castles and the remembered environment of youth takes on legendary proportion.

European fairy tales originated in personal experience in the first instance. We may like to think of them as having descended from the magical dream time of eternity, but they have not. Fairy tales have always been grounded in social, political and psychological reality, capturing real life events and couching them in allegory and metaphor – often in order that the tale-tellers were not discovered speaking the unspeakable.

Practical Method: The Fairy Tale

In this exercise, the client is asked to translate the personal autobiography into a fairy tale. The client is asked to take the characters and events of the autobiography and amplify them to mythical proportion. The client is encouraged to think allegorically and to translate their personal story into a tale which carries transpersonal implications.

It is often helpful for the practitioner to relate aspects of the autobiographies read by some group members to parts of well-known fairy tales, inspiring the client to make connections between the personal and the archetypal.

Again, to help the client focus it is useful to suggest that they set aside specific writing periods – usually an hour per day for one or two weeks. The client may use the first set of writing hours to draft the story and the latter periods to rewrite and make the editorial alterations and adjustments which bring the fairy tale to fruition.

The following are excerpts from the fairy tales written by Vicky and Richard.

Client's Fairy Tale: Vicky

The Castle of Glue

Once upon a time there was a little girl called Stuck who lived with her parents: King Tyrant and Queen Absent.

The family lived in a castle with many stairs and whenever anyone ascended or descended the stairs, the wooden boards would creak and echo throughout the castle corridors so everybody knew that someone was on the way up or on the way down.

The little girl was very unhappy because her mother was always away. She said that she had important business to do but Stuck knew that she was a

Prince Chaser and that her business consisted of luring young princes into her grasp whereupon she would kiss them to death. Queen Absent loved kissing but never once kissed Stuck and this made Stuck feel very much unloved...

Because Queen Absent was away so much, King Tyrant ruled the castle and had some very strange ideas about what was good for little girls. Often, in the middle of the night or in the middle of the day, Stuck would be sitting in her parlour crying and wishing that her mother would come home and she would hear the floorboards creak as King Tyrant ascended the stairs.

She could hear the fuming and the steaming of the King's breath as her parlour door opened and the King entered carrying his kettle of glue. Stuck had seen the kettle of glue many times and hated it. In fact, just the sight of it made her bones cold.

'Now come along,' the King said. 'Lie upon your bed and open your mouth as I have shown you to do.'

The little girl knew that she could not disobey the King, for his hands were like a lion's jaws and he could easily lift her from the floor and throw her onto her bed.

When Stuck was on her bed and her mouth was open the King climbed up on to the eiderdown with her, rested his knees, which were like the trunks of trees, upon her arms and poured the glue from the kettle into her mouth. Stuck wanted to cry and scream but she could not. She just lay helpless as she felt the glue trickle down into her throat.

After the King had finished the pouring he left the room and descended the stairs and Stuck knew when it was safe to move because the bottom stair had a creaking sound that was deeper than all the rest. So when she was sure that King Tyrant had reached the bottom of the stairs she would cry and try to wash away the glue with water. But by then most of it had set hard in her throat.

King Tyrant came to Stuck's parlour with a kettle of glue many times and, as the years passed, Stuck's throat had so much glue in it that her voice became stuck.

Then, one day, King Tyrant was killed in an accident with his horse and at the funeral all the kings and queens and princes and princesses from all the surrounding lands said what a great man he had been. Stuck found this hard to hear because she knew that he was really a wicked man who liked to hurt children with his kettle of glue. So Stuck decided that she would tell everybody the truth about King Tyrant. However, when she opened her mouth to tell the truth, her voice would not make any sound for it was covered with so much glue. Whenever Stuck tried to tell her story, people would look at her as if she was dumb as she gurgled and babbled.

So Stuck began a journey in search of a witch or wizard, a sorcerer or a seer who could find the magic potion that would unstick her voice so that she could let everybody know the truth about King Tyrant...

Client's Fairy Tale: Richard

The Bird and the Brigadier

There was once a brave Brigadier whose voice boomed and whose heart pounded with certainty and prowess. The Brigadier knew he was clever, he knew he was smart and he knew that everybody else knew that he was clever and smart.

The Brigadier's voice was loud as a foghorn and whenever he spoke people would listen to every word; and whenever he sung people would listen to every note.

The Brigadier was such an important man that everybody wanted him to visit their land so that he could speak to them with his loud and clever voice. So the Brigadier befriended a great white bird called Stability. Whenever the Brigadier needed to go to another land to sound his voice, he would mount the great white bird called Stability and fly through the sky. So confident was the Brigadier that the bird was stable that he would not bother to hold on to the bird's wings but would busy himself drinking a special potion called Vidker that loosened and lubricated his voice.

But one day, whilst Brigadier was flying the great white bird and drinking his Vidker, a storm came and tossed the bird asunder and the bird and the Brigadier came crashing down to earth.

Now this crash so frightened the Brigadier that whenever he came to open his mouth to speak or sing again, nothing came out but a faint and silly squawk.

The Power of the Telling

In writing their fairy tale, clients often discover that they can express vividly some of the more contentious and disconcerting aspects of their story with greater courage than the literal documentary of their autobiography permits.

In play therapy, children can often speak indirectly about troublesome concerns by creating an allegorical scenario with toys. The fairy tale acts in the same way, enabling the client to speak indirectly about issues which may be too embarrassing, disturbing or shameful to declare in the literal form of autobiographical disclosure.

Usually, in group work, during the reading of the fairy tales, the witnessing group are engaged on many levels. Emotionally, the group members are moved to a new level of feeling as they hear the images from the autobiographies amplified – as though the figurative amplification of the image within the tale yields an amplification of empathic affect in the audience. But simultaneously, the group will usually listen with an intrigue and a fascination as though engaged in witnessing an artistic event. In this regard, the teller is no longer fellow client or patient but performer, artist, tale-teller, story-maker and source of inspiration. As each person reads their tale, so each person experiences this emergent artist within and begins to taste its healing power. It is a shift of self-image from client to artist and the search for healing is to some extent redirected inwards towards the persons's own creative resources.

Having arrived at the fairy tale from the autobiography, the next stage is to find a new artistic form which will provide a container and a context for the amplified imagery and affect and enable clients to intensify the expression of the emotions associated with the origin of the tale whilst simultaneously evolving the artistic process of creativity. This next stage involves transforming fairy tale into song and unearthing the healing power of singing.

CHAPTER 3

Priests, Bards and Shamans
A Brief History of Singing and Healing

In Ancient Greece

For centuries, the most consistently revered form of singing in the west has been that displayed by the opera singer, whose virtuosity and skill exemplifies for many the most highly developed form of vocal expression. This operatic vocalisation originates in ancient Greece, where lone players told the tales of the great myths accompanying themselves with a small stringed instrument called a lyre and where they played all of the characters, giving each one a distinctive vocal quality whilst retaining a neutral voice for the narration. In time, these solo renditions developed into small ensemble performances; and later playwrights wrote the mythical stories in dialogue form and small groups of players came together and played one or two characters each. In the process of transition from solo recitals in story and music to actual musical and dramatic productions, the use of the mask was added and the vocal dance of word and song emerged from the actor through a hole cut into the mask at the mouth. The etymology of our term 'personality' is inextricably linked to this use of the human voice and originates in these masked performances. The term 'personality' comes from the Latin *per sona* which means 'the sound passes through' and was first used to describe the mouthpiece of the mask worn by actors. It then came to denote the character or person which the actor portrayed. Eventually the word came to mean any person, and finally 'personality' as we now understand it.

The new masked theatre productions became one of the most significant contributions which the Greeks made to Europe's future cultural and artistic development; moreover, it was from one of these plays that Freud drew his theory of the Oedipus Complex; it was these performances that inspired Aristotle and Plato to speculate their philosophy of art and the nature of human emotions; and it was in turn from these philosophies that Freud drew the concept of 'catharsis'.

Aristotle proposed the theory that the audience who witness the performances of the mythical tragedies experience the fate of the central character intensely, as though it were their own. In particular, he hypothesised that the onlookers feel immense pity for the character's predicament and extreme fear in imagining that such a fate might befall them. According to Aristotle, such active investment of belief in the theatre of tragedy gave rise to a means by which the audience could purge themselves of the affects of pity and fear and thereby experience a genuine psychological relief which he called *catharsis*. It was from these ideas concocted to describe the psychological effect of theatre that Freud drew the term 'cathartic method' which he originally used to describe his 'talking cure'.

The plays of this cathartic theatre were performed by three or four actors who played the main characters and a group of performers known as the chorus who sang, yelled, spoke and chanted in a powerful and exuberant mixture of prayer and narration, serving to work the actors and the audience into a climactic state. Many of the texts from these plays still exist as do many vivid descriptions of the productions by ancient philosophers, historians and politicians who attended them. From these extant writings we know that the actors and chorus recited their dialogue not in a fashion analogous with daily speech, but with special intonations which were accentuated by the music of a lyre or a flute-like instrument called an aulos. The bodily movements used by the performers were also stylised, forming a choreographed gestural dance which contributed to the overall arousing effect which the spectacle is known to have had on the audience. To the modern ear this acoustic aspect of Greek theatre would probably sound chaotic and lacking in all melody. There was no concept of musical harmony and the utterances of the voice, pipes and strings served the purpose not of articulating the formal discursive logic of a musical composition but of enhancing the text with exhilarating emotive sounds. We know that the Greeks did not create combinations of voice and instruments which a modern ear would describe as concordant. Although such combinations as we might call harmonious may have occurred spontaneously in the course of playing, it would not have been possible to plan it or fix it from one performance to the next because their system of writing music down was not sophisticated enough. The Greeks simply used the letters of their own alphabet to indicate notes on their scale, with some letters turned around to denote changes in the quality of a sound. When the

Romans infiltrated and overpowered Greek culture, they simply exchanged the signs of Greek notation for their own alphabet, but did not significantly elaborate its complexity.

Every play in Greek drama incorporates a spectrum of inarticulate sounds which express grief, fear, joy or triumph and other emotions through vocal sobs, groans, screams, gasps, laughs and ululations. These sounds are of supreme importance for the emotional effects of Greek tragedy, initiating physical and emotional vibrations which served the climactic atmosphere; though of course, editors often ignore them and translators are commonly satisfied with recording them as a perfunctory 'oh', 'ah', or 'alas'.

The use of the voice in Greek theatre was clearly acrobatic and extensive, serving to communicate emotions of extreme magnitude, the effect of which was to arouse the passions of the audience to a high degree of excitation in order that they might experience a catharsis. Indeed the term 'audience' comes from *audio*, meaning 'I hear'. In ancient Greece then, theatre was closely related to therapy by way of its cathartic effect; to the Greeks, the art of theatre was by its very nature medicinal, and they held music in the same regard. In Greek mythology, music and medicine were literally sister and brother. The Muses were divine characters who invented music and reigned over its human use and Aesculapius was the inventor of medicine capable even of raising people from the dead. Both the Muses and Aesculapius were fathered by Apollo and their charms were equally revered as being capable of affecting the health of mortals. Apollo was thus regarded as the father of medicine and of music and it was Apollo's son Orpheus who came to be regarded as the keeper of the mysteries of song and its healing powers. In the myth of Orpheus, when the hero descends into the underworld to rescue his beloved, he discovers that the power of his singing voice can pacify any aggressor including Hades himself.

To the ancient Greeks, who were inspired particularly by Pythagoras, the fundamental principles of music, such as rhythm, melody and proportion of high and low, soft and loud, all had their equivalent in the human soul or psyche. The right music could therefore bring the soul into order and integration whilst the wrong sounds could throw the whole person into confusion, madness and disarray. During Roman times, Cicero, in the tradition of Pythagoras, proclaimed that every emotion had a corresponding vocal sound and he compared the tones of the voice to the strings of the lyre, both of which he believed could be tuned to represent perfectly changes in human mood and temperament. Later still, during the Renaissance, the notion of a soul-map for the voice was further developed into principles for the composition of vocal music. Renaissance composers took the four elements of earth, water, air and fire, originally depicted by the Greek philosopher Hippocrates, and equated them with different classical vocal ranges. Earth was bass, water was tenor, alto was air and soprano was fire. Each of the Hippocratic elements was thought to correspond respectively to four humours in the body: blood, phlegm, yellow bile and black bile, the balance between which was thought to be crucial for the healthy functioning of the body. Vocal music was thus composed in such a way as to create a harmonious and proportionate combination of the four vocal timbres and thus induce an analogous equilibrium in the corresponding humours of the body.

Enter the Romans

The Romans inherited from the Greeks the use of music and drama as a form of mass public entertainment which formed an important part of pre-Christian Roman life. However, with the coming of Christianity these great pagan tales of raging gods and supreme heroes, whose deeds were emulated in action with mask and song to the awe and wonder of the adoring masses, disappeared. Worship and admiration for the ways of the deity took on a more solemn form. An important part of the solemnity which is associated with early Christian worship is the way in which holy scripture was uttered in such sorrowful and non-elaborate tones by the church leaders and worshippers alike. This was indeed a far cry from the spectacular vocal renditions which the Greeks gave of their religious stories.

It was the pre-Christian Romans who invented the organ, originally a contraption about ten feet high and four and a half feet wide – blown by means of a weight of water whilst the later ones were air-blown by hand. And, although those of the Christian church did not choose to inherit the revelries and masked dramas from their pre-Christian antecedents, they did retain the organ and by about 350 BC the first singing schools were established in Europe to train singers to give voice to the words of God in timely synonymity with the authoritative solemnity of the organ. By this time the organs had become gigantic affairs and required two or three players, called 'organ beaters', to thump the huge keys with gloved hands whilst a group of 'blowers' pumped the bellows. But the simultaneous combination of organ and choral singers was still a far cry from what later became known as harmony.

As a result of these musical experiments with voice and organ, which had no system of notation capable of restraining the impromptu expression of feeling on any pitch, the once solemn chants became more elaborate and often quite vigorous and the church authorities believed this to be incompatible with the reverence due to God. As a result, the church made strict rules dictating the kinds of vocal sounds and combinations thereof which could and could not be used.

It was from this desire on the part of the clergy to control the nature of the singing voice that the first singing schools of Europe sprang. Among the most renowned was that implemented by Pope Sylvester in the early part of the fourth century who established a musical conservatory, the *Schola Cantorum*, where the principles of tone production and musical theory were taught to ordained singers. With the passage of time the specific demands and taboos of the church with regard to the singing voice became more conservative and stipulations demanding what could and could not be sung culminated in the infamous rulings of Pope Gregory the Great, during the second half of the sixth century, whose strict stipulations led to the Gregorian chant which is still in use.

Systematic instruction in the art of singing therefore originally served the process of ordaining those who could perform the musical services of the church according to its taste. The presence of a trained élite at the service naturally put the spontaneous vocalisations of the congregation to shame and in 350 AD the Laodiciean Council and later the fourth Council of Carthage decreed that congregational singing interfered with the beauty of the musical service as held up by the trained singers and rules were drawn up to limit the participation in the service by the congregation.

Singing Shamans

During the so-called dark ages which followed the collapse of the Roman Empire in western Europe during the sixth century, lone players continued to roam the lands singing and telling their own stories with the aid of music. These singing tale-tellers who owed their birth to the ancient Greeks and who remained untouched by the demands of the church, were to become a significant part of European song culture. The most well known of these are perhaps the troubadours, singing poets who flourished in southern France throughout the twelfth, thirteenth and fourteenth centuries and whose wandering lives full of passion and adventure made them the typical romantic figures of their age. But the troubadours are only one example of the many kinds of singers and poets who wandered alone and in groups throughout Europe combining story, text and music to entertain in the courts, in the taverns and on the streets.

Many cultures have, at various times in history, hosted travelling or local artists whose function was to keep myth, mystery and indigenous religious tradition alive through the oral expression of tale, narrative, parable and song; and in many cases their function was also a healing one. The general term for such persons is 'bard', who in more recent history have been seen as mere entertainers but who stem from a shamanic tradition where mystical knowledge of the myths and insight into rituals of healing, combined with the artistic skill of the singer and reciter were contained in a single person. In many ways, the bard is the precedent for the healing artists of today. Whilst in French they were the troubadours, in Africa they were *griots*, in Norse they were *skalds*, in Anglo-Saxon they were *gleemen*, in Russian they were the *kaleki*, in India the *magahda* and in Japanese the *zenza*. Originally, these singers healed mind and body with a musical medicine. But, in many cultures, the bardic tradition eventually became one of entertainment, losing its original connection to the priestly virtue of imparting mystical truths to the listeners through the palatable and accessible form of musical song.

In most cultures then, the singer was a sorcerer and seer before he became an artist; and the roots of oral traditional narrative are not artistic but spiritual in the broadest sense. Indeed, it was the bard or the 'singer of tales' who preserved not only a shamanic healing tradition in many indigenous cultures, but who, in the European tradition, also preserved the great mythical epics such as Beowulf, the Iliad and the Odyssey.

In many indigenous cultures that have been relatively untouched by the ways of western medicine, the use of vocal sounds to heal the sick is or was often the guarded practice of a select member of the community – a medicine woman, a magician, a sorcerer, a witch doctor or a shaman; and one of the significant similarities between the rituals of all cultures with a shamanic content is the role played by the human voice in the process of healing.

In cultures where the medicinal services of shamans or other chosen individuals have been or still are employed, the process of healing is intimately connected with belief in a spiritual cause for physical illness, and the treatment issued by the healer is aimed not at allaying the physical symptom but at ridding the body and soul of the spirits which are thought to be its cause.

Central to the act of spiritual exorcism by which the shaman flushes causative evil from the sick patient is the process of catharsis by which the patient discharges pestilent and violating spirits and emotions and is thereby purified; and these bottled-up fragments of emotion and spirit often emerge in the form of terrifying vocal noises which the patient emits whilst in a state of semi-consciousness. In cultures where trance and spirit possession play a role in the religious, ritual and curative process, song and non-verbal utterance are often central to the curative process. Sometimes the utterance is emitted using a vocal emission totally different from the ordinary singing voice representative of a particular culture; such vocal sounds often have no articulate words but are a string of syllables, cries, screeches and improvised sonic forms which sustain the trance experience. In shamanism, this spiritual aspect to disease brings a religious dimension to the healing process in which the healer is not the objective and detached representative of science, but an active participant in the liaison between the earthly life of the patient and the spiritual world. This means that the shaman must sometimes take the evil spirits from the patient into his own body and later coax them out through a self-exorcism.

One of the most crucial gifts of the spirit world to the shaman is the song which is believed to be the lost language of the animals that everyone could speak long ago. Such shamanic songs, which have a therapeutic role, often accompany the summoning of a guardian spirit or may express the search for union with a particular animal considered to possess a special quality of power. During healing ceremonies, the shaman usually dances deliriously, singing the healing songs and uttering piercing cries or chanting a maniacal and indecipherable spirit language. Often, such rituals are aided by an onlooking audience who enforce the atmosphere of climactic purgation by chanting, yelling, sobbing and screaming. All of this contributes to a cathartic experience which is often central to shamanic ritual.

The culture of the American Indians, for example, has a long history of using voice and song as an integral part of their healing rituals. In many of the northern tribes part of the cure for illness involves finding the person who knows the correct song appropriate to a particular illness. These medicine songs come to certain 'chosen ones' in special prophetic dreams which warn of the havoc that will be wreaked by the coming of a particular disease. Often the singing of these songs is accompanied by the ritual chanting of the whole family to the rhythmic beat of a rattle held by the medicine man. Only by remembering and guarding the life-long existence of the song can the dreamer protect the tribe from impending destruction and these songs are therefore preserved by being passed down orally through the generations.

But it is not only amongst the American Indians that singing forms or has once formed part of the curative rituals for disease. Anthropologists report the medicinal use of music, song and voice in many indigenous peoples including the tribes of Papua New Guinea, the nomadic peoples of the Sahara and the Sudan as well as the Aborigines of Australia, where among the Wurajeri peoples, the process by which a novice becomes a doctor includes having a spirit companion 'sung into' him by an elder. This 'singing transmission' enables the power of the elder to duplicate itself in the novice, enhancing the latter's power without depleting that of the former. Among the medicine men of the Yamana of Tierra del Fuego, singing also plays a crucial role in initiation practices where only through vocalisation can an initiate acquire the power of a healer and activate his shamanic soul.

These examples of a shamanic tradition represent a small vestige of what was once a worldwide phenomenon which effected healing through the power of singing.

Sounds of Contemplation

Parallel to the shamanic tradition of vocal healing is the contemplative tradition of prayer and meditation where the voice plays an important role in assisting spiritual purification and psychosomatic curation. The human voice is used to such an end in traditions where singing or chanting sits at the centre of a religious or esoteric discipline, such as that practised within Tibetan Buddhism and that originating in Mongolia. In both of these traditions, the singer is able to sound two notes at once by humming or singing a single pitch whilst altering the shape and size of the oral cavity, thus varying the harmonic spectrum of a single note. Among these harmonics is often a very high overtone which is as piercing and shrill as the fundamental is basal and dark.

Among the chants most recognisable to contemporary ears is that which accompanies a Buddhist meditation and which consists of repetitious utterance of the sound OM. Such focused vocalisation is also widely pursued in Indian Hindu contexts where the chanting articulates a mantra, that is a Sanskrit prayer, and the repetition of the mantra, often on a single tone, awakens the spirit and its ability to facilitate contemplation.

The Sanskrit chanting is connected to a perception of the human body quite different from the western allopathic body-map. The body is perceived as containing centres or wheels of energy spaced vertically parallel to the spinal column. These wheels, known in Sanskrit as *chakras*, each have a specific quality of energetic fabric and each effect the functioning of specific bodily parts and organs. These chakras underpin the system of breath and movement work known as *yoga*.

The chakras are connected to each other by fine threads or routes of energetic matter called *nadis* and each main chakra is associated with a major nerve plexus and an endocrine gland. Consequently, according to this view, blockage or impedance in the flow of energy through the nadis or problems with the receptivity and energetic permeability of the chakras can result in general spiritual and emotional disturbance as well as physiological pathology in a specific endocrine gland, nerve plexus or organ directly associated with it. In Hindu and yogic literature the unique source which activates the energy of the chakras and assists in the awakening of higher consciousness is called the *Kundalini*, which in Sanskrit means 'coiled serpent'. This snake lies at the bottom of the chakra system in the region of the first chakra, in many people sleeping and dormant. However, when the snake is awakened, the energy rises up through the chakras, passing through each one and facilitating enlightenment and higher consciousness.

The most widely practised means to achieve this awakening and rising of energy is that of meditation, which, when practised regularly over a long period of time causes the chakras to open and clear, from the root upwards to the crown. One of the means to achieve this meditation is through vocalisation and in the Hindu chanting, certain sounds stimulate and purify the chakras, serving not only to awaken the soul and the spirit but to awaken the body's energetic and spiritual aspiration to health.

An aspect shared by many non-western approaches to healing is the concept of 'energy', a vital life force which can be activated through song, voice and chant. In Sanskrit this is known as *prana*; in Chinese it is *chi*; in Japanese it is *ki*; in Tibetan it is *thig-le* or *rlung*. For example, another body-map which relies upon a flow of energy through certain key points is the ancient Chinese system which perceives a flow of an energy known as *chi* through pathways known as meridians which have nexus points around the body and which are utilised in acupuncture and acupressure. The chi energy, which is perceived as physically and spiritually nutrient, enters the body at the acupuncture points and seeps deeper into the organs of the body. There are 12 pairs of meridians linked to specific organ systems. When the flow of the chi becomes blocked at or near a particular acupuncture point, the relevant organ system to that point becomes dysfunctional or diseased.

Thus, though entirely different in modality and form, both the ecstatic shamanic tradition and the contemplative meditative tradition are founded upon a fundamental belief in the relationship between vocal sound, spiritual well-being and psychosomatic healing.

Meanwhile in Europe

Whilst in non-western cultures, spiritual practice and healing found sisterhood in vocal expression through shamanic and contemplative activities, music became increasingly formalised in the west and lost its connection with therapeutic and spiritual intentions.

Around the sixth century AD the crude system of alphabetical notation which had been originated by the Greeks was superseded by a system of points, hooks, curves and lines placed above the words to be sung. These signs, called 'neumes', became formalised so that to a trained singer each had its own meaning. By this means it was possible to recall melodies already committed to memory, but it still did not enable previously unheard songs to be learnt, as the notation did not indicate pitch. It was not until around the end of the ninth and beginning of the tenth century that the pitch of musical notes began to be fixed by notation. However, there was still a long way to go before the God-fearing men of the cloth were satisfied that the resulting sound was in tune with their Master's wishes and in the year 1020 a learned Benedictine Monk called Guido of Arezzo wrote that 'in the church service it often sounds not as if we were praising God but rather as if we were engaging in quarrelling amongst ourselves'.

Guido set out to remedy this lack of harmonious concord amongst worshipping vocalists by developing the system of notation which was to give birth to the well-known tonic scale still in use: doh-ray-me-fah-soh-la-te-doh. Guido's success in creating the four line stave and fixing a named scale of notes has led him to be known as the father of literate music as we now know it.

The founding of this scale had and continues to have an insidious yet dominating effect on the art of singing training and on the accessibility of song for many people. For it made singing training irreversibly synonymous with musical training, an equation still visible today in the fact that singing teachers almost invariably work through the medium of set literately notated music. Moreover, it is impossible for a student to enter any of the major western training schools or conservatories to study singing without the ability to read music. The fact that musical literacy has become an unquestioned prerequisite for training in western culture is a testimony to our cultural arrogance and sense of supremacy for, in the vast majority of the remaining world, singing is not related to any kind of literacy at all. In the west, however, singing lessons and the act of singing are terrifying and often inaccessible notions and vast numbers of people feel alienated from training their singing voices because they do not have a so-called aptitude for or ability to read music. Musical instinct has been sequestered and subsumed by musical literacy. Yet, in its origin, singing in Europe was a dramatic use of the voice to articulate story without regard for scale or fixed melody.

The Genesis of Opera

Around the ninth century, the Christian Church began to introduce music and drama into its services where Easter Passions and Christmas Nativities which contained spoken text and sung choruses became a part of Christian ceremony throughout Europe. The origin of the idea of a religious story told in music, speech and song, which constituted the fundamental concept of these Christian performances, is rooted in the ancient history of Greece. But the formal structuring of music, which was developed primarily in the hands of the church, completely altered the way that the voice was used. In Greek tragedy it was unbound by fixed musicality and served instead to encapsulate the emotional tones, rhythms and atmospheres of the myth being played. In Christian service however, the voice now served to articulate the written score which was attached to the words arbitrarily and in a manner completely dislocated from the emotive impulse generated by the utterance of the word.

However, in Italy towards the end of the sixteenth century there lived an influential man of music, Giovanni de' Bardi, the Count of Vernio, who invited to his house the most celebrated and learned men of music and letters where they gathered to form a society of fellows whose shared aim was to rediscover the way in which the ancient Greeks had used voice, movement, music and drama in their theatre. It was from the meetings of this exclusive musical society called the *Camerata*, which took place over a period of 30 years in seventeenth-century Florence, that opera as people know it today was born. When Count Bardi moved to Rome in 1592 the meeting place of the Camerata changed to the house of the younger Jacopo Corsi who kept his house open like a public academy for all those interested in the liberal arts. It was here in 1598 that what is considered to be the first true opera was performed. The opera was called *Dafne*, with music composed by Peri.

Peri was convinced that the ancient Greeks had used a form of vocal expression more musical than that of ordinary speech but less melodious than song as the church had conceived of it, to produce an intermediate form. Peri was aiming for something between the slow and suspended movements of song and the swift and rapid movements of speech and said that he wanted to 'imitate speech in song' and use 'elegances and graces' that cannot be notated.

Amongst the members of the Camerata was the great vocal soloist Giulio Caccini who became the academy's authority on solo singing technique. Caccini was also inspired by his belief that the ancient Greeks had possessed a natural ability to express human emotions through the voice and he combined this with his development of fixed notated musical composition. The aim of his teaching was to nurture singers to bring full expression to the portrayal of human emotions whilst retaining musical harmony with the supporting instruments. It was from this objective of Caccini and others that the school of composers and singers known as Bel Canto arose.

'Bel Canto' is an Italian term which literally means 'beautiful song' and was the particular art of singing and vocal training which flourished in Italy throughout the seventeenth and eighteenth centuries in response to the need for emotional genuineness and authenticity combined with musical precision and virtuosity. Bel Canto singing was passed on through the classic singing schools of Florence, Rome, Naples, Bologna and Milan though the term 'Bel Canto' was not used until towards the end of the nineteenth century.

The special art of the Bel Canto singers consisted in their ability to communicate a genuine expression of human emotion by singing precisely notated musical phrases with a wide range of qualities or timbres, spanning a vocal range of three octaves without losing refinement and eloquence of verbal diction. Unlike more recent classical singing for the opera, where the singer is trained to specialise in or is restricted to a single timbral quality, the Bel Canto singer could sing a vast array of qualities, covering tenor, baritone, soprano and mezzo soprano, for example. A Bel Canto voice had to be moulded in infinite degrees, passing through all the colours of the sound prism.

The core principle of the Bel Canto technique rests in the malleability and articulation of the resonating spaces above the vocal folds, particularly the pharynx. The shape of the vocal tract, which acts like an elastic tube, influences the timbre of the sound made by vibrating vocal folds. By nurturing the maximum malleability of this tube, acquiring the ability to lengthen and shorten it as well as controlling its diameter, the Bel Canto singers produced a panoply of timbres which could represent the full canvas of human emotion. It is this articulation of the vocal tract that gives rise to the set of vocal timbres which form part of the Voice Movement Therapy system of voice training, profile and analysis which I have developed and which I have described in detail elsewhere (Newham 1997b, 1998, 1999). The internal movement of the vocal tract during vocalisation can also be seen by means of a fibre optic camera passed through the nasal passages and into the larynx as shown on the video *Shouting for Jericho* (Newham 1997a).

The Discovery of the Vocal Folds

The emphasis on the malleability of the vocal tract which underpinned Bel Canto teaching was countermanded by an alternative focus on the significance of the vocal folds. Leonardo da Vinci was one of the first to attempt to analyse the larynx which he did by extracting respiratory tracts from cadavers. But it was the French anatomist, Antoine Ferrein, who discovered, while dissecting corpses in 1741, two 'shelves' in the larynx and assumed that the human voice was caused by their vibration induced by air being blown forward from the lungs like bellows. He named these shelves the *cordes vocales* and his discovery of the production of vocal sound received widespread recognition. This attention drawn to the vocal folds as the most significant aspect in the production of vocal tone contributed to the erosion of Bel Canto techniques, which had been concerned with the elasticity of the resonating spaces.

Manuel Vicente del Popolo Garcia was a great singer and singing teacher who trained his son in the Bel Canto style but treated him harshly, beating him and degrading him regularly. While his sisters became famous for their singing, Manuel Garcia junior was a failure. Seeking to find the answers to his own failure he took up the vocal fold theory of Ferrein and conducted some experiments on the larynxes of poultry in which he produced sounds with bellows. Inspired by the sight of a dentist using a mirror he constructed a contraption by which he could observe his own vocal folds. Although he had not received fame as a singer, he now became famous as the inventor of the laryngascope, a small metal instrument which is placed in the mouth and enables the larynx and vocal folds to be observed.

When his father died in 1832, Manuel Garcia junior took on the role of director of his father's singing school assuming, without justification, a reputation for being a great singing teacher. By 1856 he was so famous that his methods, by now articulated in widely disseminated books, became acknowledged as the finest in Europe.

The decline of Bel Canto may be attributed in part to Ferrein and Garcia who, with a dangerously small and historically premature knowledge of laryngeal function, abandoned the intuitive and emotional insight of the anatomically blind singers. But another reason why the emphasis on flexibility of vocal characteristics or timbres was not to last long in the development of opera was because composers began to demand voices specialised in one particular quality of sound. Operas were written which contained the demand for one voice high as a nightingale and another low as a bear, both with precise musical phrases; and from this development came the operatic specialisations of soprano, mezzo, contralto, tenor, baritone and bass.

Whilst the Bel Canto singers were intent on mastering the arts of extending the different possible emotive qualities and imagistic characteristics on each note, later singers have sought to specialise in the perfection of a single operatic quality of voice and have been loath to try and extend the range associated with it. Furthermore, the increasingly elaborate complexity of musical composition has led to a process of training operatic singers which has become more influenced by the technical demands of the music and less connected to the primal and fundamental role of the voice as the expression of emotion, narrative and experience.

From Talking Cure to Singing Cure

The history of the development of the singing voice in the west is one which charts a change from the use of the voice as an expression of emotion, narrative and tale to a use of the voice which is subservient to a formal system of logic born from the stipulations of religious hierarchy. Inherent in a therapeutic use of voice is an attempt to reverse this process and facilitate an environment where clients can discover an instinctive musicality with which to give artistic expression to their own tales.

It may seem at first that there is no connection between the roots of singing in the west and the roots of psychotherapy. Yet the connection is in fact a vital one.

Sigmund Freud initiated the practice of psychoanalysis which in turn brought about the profession of psychotherapy, a form of medicine in which the cure is contained by the words which the patient speaks. Freud discovered the Talking Cure. Indeed, psychotherapy is as much a study of language as it is of the psyche. For, central to the modality of psychotherapy is the process by which the client or patient gives voice to thought, feeling, fantasy and fact. It is an act of vocalisation and audition.

The most common complaint amongst Freud's early patients in the late nineteenth century consisted of bodily pains for which there appeared to be no physiological explanation. These included headaches, paralysed limbs, stomach upsets, respiratory problems and disturbances of speech, sight and hearing. Freud claimed to have discovered that the cause of these 'phantom diseases' usually consisted of a psychological trauma which the patient had experienced in the past, in some cases many years prior to the occurrence of the physical problem which had brought her to the doctor. Indeed, quite frequently it was a distressing childhood event, the emotional effects of which continued to disturb the patient long after it had apparently been forgotten.

Freud referred to these patients as hysterics: those in whom the emotional reaction or affect provoked by a specific psychological trauma had been converted into a physical symptom which persisted for many years afterwards. The hysteric seemed genuinely unable to recollect the precipitating event and had no idea of the causal connection between it and the bodily dysfunction.

Freud identified two distinct processes by which psychological trauma became converted into physical symptoms. The first process occurred when a person experienced a particular mental trauma whilst suffering from a genuine physiological disease. Although the person recovered from the disease, the physical symptoms recurred whenever he or she was reminded of the traumatic event which originally accompanied it. Let us take, for example, someone suffering from the severe stomach pains caused by appendicitis during which time the person suffers the mental trauma of being bereft of a close relative, which naturally arouses a strong affect of grief. If this person has a 'hysterical disposition' he or she may continue to experience the stomach pains whenever grief is aroused by new situations involving a bereavement, even long after the appendix has been removed. In such an example, a physical symptom originally generated by organic causes is later revived as an expression of a psychological affect, simply because by chance they originally occurred simultaneously.

The second process involved the patient's unwitting translation of a verbal phrase from its metaphorical into its literal meaning. For example, a traumatic event which morally disgusts and is abhorred by the patient may precipitate sporadic fits of vomiting because the linguistic term 'to be sick' is translated from its metaphorical description of psychological disgust into its literal designation of vomiting. A man who is being continually pressurised by his colleague to agree to a transaction that he feels is suspect and dubious may begin to suffer from numbness in his arm, because his work partner is metaphorically 'twisting his arm' over the deal. A 'slap in the face' describes both a severe facial neuralgia and the affect of a swiping insult; feeling choked describes both respiratory constriction about the larynx, and the affect of deep sadness. By converting such linguistic metaphors into a literal somatic experience the hysteric could genuinely feel severe spinal pain when people 'got his back up', experience agonising shooting pains in the fore-limbs when colleagues 'twisted his arm' over an issue at work, or be caused to vomit when morally disgusted. Hysterical patients therefore possessed a particular susceptibility to the power of suggestion or imagination. Through careful aural observation of the patient's speech, Freud noticed that many linguistic phrases which patients used to describe physical symptoms at the same time denoted emotional responses; this provided the key to the precipitating trauma.

Freud believed that in both processes the persistence of the bodily symptom was caused by the patient's insufficient active emotional reaction to the original event or scene, which had consequently become 'strangulated' or 'bottled up'. Freud compared the psyche to an electrical system which becomes charged with a certain amount of energy when it is affected by an event. For example, a patient who is insulted becomes excited in such a way as to increase the amount of energy in the nervous system. In healthy situations this increase in energy is immediately expended by the individual's responsive reactions which can be verbal or physical, such as a bout of abusive swearing or a histrionic waving of fists. Freud described such active responses as 'motor activity' because they were stimulated by the neurological impulses of the motor neurons which stem from the central nervous system; the function of such activity was to bring the energy level of the psyche back to a state of balance or neutrality. If, however, for reasons of social prohibition or personal inhibition, the individual represses the response, refrains from responsive motor activity and retains the increased energetic excitation, it becomes bottled up and seeks expression by converging upon a weak spot localised in a part of the body. Freud described the ideal expenditure of increased energy through motor activity in response to the original event as 'abreaction' and proposed that the physical symptoms of hysteria were the result of the emotional affect having been insufficiently abreacted.

Freud proposed that he had discovered a method of curing the somatic disease by helping the patient to remember the original upsetting experience which had accompanied the genesis of the physical symptom. This involved a thorough psycho-archaeological excavation of the patient's past in search of a single precipitating trauma which, when remembered and articulated, allegedly caused the symptom to vanish forever.

However, the somatic cure was not achieved through recollection without affect; the patient had to revive and re-enact the same intensity of emotional response to the memory of the event as was evoked by its original occurrence. Freud thus claimed to have discovered that each individual hysterical symptom immediately and permanently disappeared when he succeeded in bringing clearly to light the memory of the event by which it was provoked, in arousing its accompanying affect, in enabling the patient to describe that event in the greatest possible detail, and in successfully facilitating the client to put the emotion into words. But, most significantly, Freud asserted that the recollection of the event without emotion almost invariably produced no therapeutic result and that the event which originally took place must therefore be expressed as vividly and emotionally as possible (Freud 1953–74).

In encouraging the patients not only to verbally remember, that is to put back together the original event, but also to imbue the text of this memory with expression of the full emotional excitation which had been denied at the time of its first occurrence, Freud gave the patient a second chance to complete his reaction and in so doing release both the stored affect and along with it the somatic symptom which had hitherto served to contain it. Freud described this process of giving vent to stored-up feeling as 'catharsis', a word which he took from the effect upon the audience which Aristotle said was achieved by ancient Greek theatre. Freud thus took a term which Aristotle had used to describe the effect of an artistic event upon an audience and applied it to the effect of his Talking Cure (Freud 1953–74).

Freud proposed that the psychosomatic dysfunction came to an end as soon as the patient had spoken about it. Even if the original abreaction would normally have involved a muscular or physical reaction, such as for example a punch or other kinetic display of aggression, the full abreaction could be achieved the second time around through words alone; thus, according to Freud, words are substitutes for deeds. However, because the verbal memory of the precipitating trauma had to be experienced in full emotional depth, the patient was encouraged not to remember in a cool, detached and reflective way but to speak as though he or she were experiencing it all over again. If the patient simply spoke the words which described the remembered event with no emotional recollection, the cure was ineffectual. It was, therefore, not the words alone that performed the cure, but the voice which expressed all the emotions associated with the memory through its acoustic tonal and timbral quality, ranging from sobbing to rage, from bitter grief to intimidated fear. Freud's medicine was not in fact a talking cure, but a vocal cure.

Freud forgot the artistic dimension to the cathartic experience and ignored a large part of the human voice by focusing so single-mindedly upon the spoken word. To fill our memories with emotion requires us to use the full range of our voice to express the full range of our feelings. And nowhere do we witness such a use of the voice more intensely than in the art of singing.

In Voice Movement Therapy, the original cathartic vision is transposed from a talking cure to a singing cure.

CHAPTER 4

From Fairy Tale to Song
Creating Rhapsody from the Themes of Personal Experience

The Therapeutic Art of the Ballad

A ballad is a story told in song and musicalises a narrative journey; and to sing a ballad based on one's own story brings a new therapeutic dimension to the healing process. Throughout history, people have sung of their plight, their woes and their history. And the more fraught with oppression, struggle and difficulty a group of people are, the healthier and livelier their song culture is.

No one has ever discovered a culture, a tribe or a society which does not sing. Every group of people shares a body of song: from the nomadic tribes of the Icelandic snow planes to the Aborigines of the Australian desert; from the Indians of the Peruvian forest to the Masai warriors of the Kenyan bush; from the introverted communities of the Mongolian mountains to the extroverted explorers of North America. Singing is a universal custom and the songs of a culture express its beliefs and taboos, its worries and its victories. The communal spirit of a society is preserved in song.

Singing has always been an enlivening communal activity which has brought people together in joy and in grief, in sorrow and in jubilation. At the wedding feast and in the funeral procession, in the cotton fields and along the railroads, in the gospel halls and in the chapels, among marching soldiers and protesting prisoners, among the faithful and among those who despair – singing has, since the earliest times, released people from isolation and enabled those from all quarters of the globe to make themselves known to God and to the world.

Singing implies promise of redemption. Singing inspires hope where all else fails. Singing loosens the chains of the enslaved, rattles the bars of the imprisoned, mobilises the strength of the starving and defies the domination of self-appointed oppressors. Singing gives dominion to those without territory, passes time for those who await judgement and gives voice to a part of the soul which can not be beaten, broken or beleaguered. Indentured slaves sang in the cotton fields of North America; captive hostages sang in the jails of the Middle East; Kurdish families sang as they fled across the Turkish border; British convicts sang aboard the giant vessels which transported them to Australia; teenage soldiers joined with their enemies to sing Christmas carols in the snow-drenched trenches of the First World War; abandoned children have sung themselves to sleep in the lonely and impersonal dormitories of their orphanage; incarcerated Jews sang to themselves in the cells of concentration camps; minorities of every persuasion have sung through nocturnal vigils outside houses of parliament and government; marching protesters have sung in defence of those who have been wrongly accused and entire communities have congregated to sing in worship of their maker. Songs are sung to commemorate victory and commiserate in defeat; songs are sung to celebrate birth, death, marriage and anniversary; songs are sung to protest against injustice, to honour achievement, to encapsulate history, to envision the future, to resound the sentiment of pride and to give form to rage and loathing. A song may speak of love and terror, crime and compassion. In song we can sing the unspeakable. There is not an emotion or thought, an instinct or desire which cannot be perfectly communicated through song.

Practical Method: The Journey Song

Having written and presented both an autobiography and a fairy tale, the client is now asked to write the lyrics for a song which encapsulates their life journey. The client is encouraged to combine the literal documentary writing style of the autobiography with the allegorical imagistic style of the fairy tale to form a third style born from the two. This third style is written as a series of lyrics which are intended to be sung; however, the client is encouraged not to consider melody at all but to concentrate only on the literary aspects.

Again, to help the client focus it is useful to suggest that they set aside specific writing periods – usually an hour per day for one or two weeks. The client may use the first set of writing hours to draft the story and the latter periods to rewrite and make the editorial alterations and adjustments which bring the journey song to fruition.

When the task is completed, the next stage offers the client an opportunity to read the lyrics of the journey song aloud to the practitioner, or in the case of group work, to the entire ensemble. The audience is asked to listen generously and not to intervene or remark in any way.

Client's Song: Vicky

Ungluing the Voice

As a child, Vicky was repeatedly abused by her father who made her engage in oral sex. Her memories were very vivid, particularly the feeling of 'a numb helplessness' in her body as her father knelt on her arms to keep her down. Vicky came to work on herself through Voice Movement Therapy because, although psychotherapy had enabled her to deal with and overcome many of the issues and heal some of the damage, some problems remained. The main problem was a feeling of tightness in her throat and what she described as 'an incredibly inhibited voice'. Whenever she came to project her voice or speak up about something important, she would feel a 'stickiness' in her throat, as though her voice was 'covered with something' that made it 'dull and unable to flow fluidly'.

After the Voice Movement Journey session in which Vicky had read excerpts from her autobiography, I had asked participants to rewrite the story as the lyrics for a song. Vicky returned with the following lyrics which she read aloud:

> Sperm and cream it makes me scream
> Daddy made me suck his big Jimmy Dean
> My arms went dead and the voice in my head
> Told me to endure this sight obscene
> I was only little with no real choice
> Oh please God let me take the glue from my voice
> I have tried to fight and punch and kick
> To expel from my mouth his big salty prick
> But the more I try the more I cry
> And I choke and spew and people wonder why
> For Dad is dead and no one gets
> Why my voice is stuck and why I seem upset
> But if I feel quite safe and no one hurts me so
> I can relax my body and I start to let go
> And when I do my voice unglues
> And I start to hear myself afresh and anew

At the end of this rendition, Vicky recalled that after an abusive episode as she lay alone on her bed, she would often sing to herself very quietly as a way of comforting herself; it was something that no one could take from her and it gave her a place to put her distress, loneliness and shame. Now she found that reading the lyrics to her song fulfilled some of the same function. It gave her a means to release the emotions associated with her ordeal but also provided a place to put them. However, she was now eager to musicalise the lyrics and sing them; and this is the next stage in the process of Voice Movement Therapy.

Client's Song: Richard

I Heard the Plane Come Down

Richard was one of a few who had survived an aeroplane crash. Though he had remarkably and miraculously not sustained any serious physical injury, the event had severe consequences regarding his mental and emotional life.

His symptoms included insomnia, nightmares, periods of extreme depression, suicidal fantasies and panic attacks. Before the accident, Richard had been an outspoken person with a loud and resonant voice. Now, his speaking voice was almost a whisper and he felt nervous when called upon to speak up for himself. Richard had come into therapy because he wanted to refind both his singing voice in order that he could rejoin a choir and his speaking voice so that he could 'begin to put his life back together'.

The only optical memory which Richard had of the plane crash was seeing the head of the person he was sitting adjacent to separate from his body. The rest was, he said 'complete darkness' until he was placed upon a stretcher by the medical team. What Richard did have was a complete spectrum of acoustic memories: engine noises, announcements of the pilot, the screams of the passengers and the sirens of the emergency team. Indeed when Richard told the story, most of his sentences which described the three minutes leading up to the point of impact – at which he became buried by debris and contained by darkness – began with the words: 'I heard'.

For example, he said 'I heard the pilot announce his apologies for the difficult take-off'; he said 'I heard the crashing of the glasses in the steward area'; he said 'I heard the sirens of the emergency team and I knew I was alive'; and he said 'I heard someone say: "It's all right we are going to get you out."'

I could not help being struck by the rhythm and tonality of the repetitious use of the motif 'I heard' which began each of his sentences. I therefore suggested to Richard that he used this motif to write the lyrics for his song. When it came to Richard's turn to read the lyrics, he read:

I heard the engine rumble

I heard the plane jolt

I heard the captain say there was a problem

I heard the passengers cry

I heard the woman behind me praying

I heard the scraping of metal on tarmac

I heard the tyres skidding

I heard sirens whistling

I heard someone ask if I could hear them

I heard the plane come down

As Richard read the words, he swayed slightly from side to side and his voice trembled as tears swelled up in his eyes. The atmosphere in the room was intense and the group was absolutely still. Afterwards Richard said, 'I need to sing this. I need to give this music.'

The Music in the Words

Oral communication between adults is composed of two dimensions: voice and speech. The term 'voice' refers to the sound produced by the vibrating vocal cords. The term 'speech' refers to the shaping of these sounds into words by articulating the mouth, lips, jaw and tongue. In fact, the term 'linguistic' comes from *lingua*, the Latin word for tongue. The sound of the voice, independent of the words uttered, is composed of different ingredients including pitch, breathiness and loudness which combine in different proportions to form a range of colours or timbres; and it is the timbre of the voice which acts as the messenger for our state of mind, moods, emotions and inner attitudes. In Voice Movement Therapy, the human voice is perceived as a composite of ten such fundamental components which combine to produce a spectrum of voice qualities and types. This system of component voice analysis is described in the following chapter and outlined briefly in Appendix 1 of this volume. It is also explained fully in the book *Therapeutic Voicework: Principles and Practice for the Use of Singing as a Therapy* (Newham 1997b) and presented on the audio course *The Singing Cure* (Newham 1998).

Most people are quite aware that the same spoken phrase can be uttered in such a variety of timbres as to communicate significantly different meanings. In the words of a common but wise adage: 'it is not what you say but the way that you say it'. But in addition to the timbre of the voice, speech is articulated with a certain prosody. Prosody is the music which underpins language, it is the rise and fall in pitch which brings attitude and implication to what we say and engages the listener in a way that monotone would not. In rare situations, a change in prosody can actually change the meaning of the words. For example, take the sentence 'Jane kissed Susan's mother and then Susan kissed her'. If you speak this so that the final word 'her' is uttered on the same note as the preceding word 'kissed', then the sentence communicates that Susan kissed her mother. However, if you say 'Jane kissed Susan's mother and then Susan kissed *her*' so that you stress the last word and utter it on a sliding scale, the sentence communicates that Susan kissed Jane. This is an example of how prosody influences meaning. Most of the time, however, prosody does not alter meaning but brings character and emotional colour to what we say. It is the music of our speech.

Although the voice may give speech its emotional meaning, it does not necessarily simply enforce the verbal content. For example, if the speaker is in some kind of personal conflict, the verbal and vocal channels may carry contradictory information. This is called incongruence and often occurs when the words we choose paint a public face which disguises our true feelings. We say that we are willing to do something for a friend with a tone of voice which reveals a reluctance to help; we say that we are 'doing fine' whilst we are actually choked with sadness. When such an incongruence between the vocal and verbal message occurs, the voice is more likely to reveal the truth about the personality than the speech.

A common kind of incongruence can often be heard in the acoustic messages conveyed to children by their parents and many clients have been raised on a staple diet of confused and ambivalent messages. As a result, they in turn can find it hard to convey a single intention or feeling. Instead, they paint one picture with the words which they speak and another with their vocal intonation.

For example, I once worked with a man whom we shall call Michael who was an only child and who had been raised by a single mother. The mother was frail, lonely and dependent upon her son for company. Whenever Michael announced that he was going out alone, to spend time with a friend or to take part in the social activities befitting his age, his mother's words would wish him well and encourage him on his way. However, her tone of voice would give Michael the impression that she really didn't want him to go. This had made it very difficult for Michael to leave his mother. Even as an adult, he felt that in some way he ought to be at home looking after her. Michael found it very difficult to be clear about his needs, particularly in his relationships with women. He would want affection but convey an attitude of cold detachment. He would wish to bring a relationship to an end, but continue to humour someone, too afraid to be clear about his feelings.

The Musical Brain

The neurological organisation of logical processes such as speaking, counting and rationalising are localised in the left hemisphere of the brain. Non-logical processes such as emotive vocal expression, artistic creativity and fantasising, meanwhile, are localised in the neurology of the right hemisphere. This is why people who have suffered a stroke may lose the ability to utilise the spoken word but can remember and sing songs. The ability to sing is dealt with by the right hemisphere, whilst language is processed by the left hemisphere. The sad thing is that singing often becomes a left hemisphere activity when people learn to read and write music. Then, rather than singing remaining an improvisational, creative act with tunes and lyrics drawn from memory and inspiration, the act of singing becomes a logical and literary operation with tunes read from the crotchets and quavers upon the page.

During the preverbal stage of development, the young infant draws upon the musical and emotional centres of the right hemisphere to call out a spontaneous and intuitive sonata of sound which gives direct expression to mood, instinct and emotion. But as the child enters verbal language, the left hemisphere begins to dominate the scene and the logical and rational code of spoken discourse replaces the aesthetic code of musical expression. In western society the powers of the left hemisphere are held in high esteem whilst the domain of the right hemisphere is considered to be less important. Children's progress is measured in terms of how readily they are able to master logical operations, even if the logic is in discrepancy with the senses. For example, two of the functions operated by the left hemisphere are that of mathematics and spatial geometry; and a child is rewarded for mastering these fields. Yet many of the conclusions formed by this framework have little to do with reality. Our senses tell us that if you drop a brick from 500cm above the ground it will hit the floor very quickly. But the maths tells us that it must first fall half the distance, bringing it 250cm from the floor, then half that distance, bringing it 125cm from the ground, then half that distance, bringing it 62.5cm from the ground and so on *ad infinitum*. According to the wisdom of left hemisphere mathematics and spatial geometry, the brick would never reach the floor but would spend forever travelling smaller and smaller distances.

In the early stages of life a child is unable to conceive that an object continues to exist when it can not be touched, seen, heard, smelled or tasted; the child's knowledge derives from the senses. However, the child gradually realises that objects continue to exist even when their presence can not be experienced. This realisation is coincident with the process of learning to name things. By attaching names and numbers to things the child can manipulate and organise the words and numerals instead of the things which they stand for. However, words are not things and numbers do not obey the reality of physical quantity. So from the moment the child becomes verbal and numerate, an abyss opens up between the intelligence of the senses and the intelligence of logic.

When we listen to music and allow it to work upon our emotions and elicit musings and fantasies from our imagination, we are drawing on the intuitive propensity of the right hemisphere; when we sing spontaneously and create improvised melodies, we are also drawing on the instinctive creativity of the right hemisphere; and when we recall a song from memory and give it voice we are again drawing on the right hemisphere. But, when we read music from the score upon the page or write our improvised melody down with crotchets and quavers, we are using the logical capacity of the left hemisphere.

Psychologists have recently uncovered some astounding facts about what happens to young children regarding these different relationships to music. First, they took many groups of children and witnessed them playing freely with their voices and with instruments, creating their own music through improvisation and describing the atmospheres, images and feelings evoked by each other's compositions. Then they split all the groups into two. One half of each group then spent several years learning to play an instrument and acquiring the ability to write and read formal music notation. Meanwhile, the second half of each group continued to explore musical improvisation without formal music training. They discovered that those who acquired the formal musical ability of the left hemisphere lost the ability to improvise and describe the emotionality of sounds, whilst those who avoided the formal training developed advanced creative skills and an acute emotional sensitivity to sound. The term for the destruction of musical intuition as a result of formal training has been called the 'wipe out effect'.

We all rely upon the musicality of our voice to express the emotional content of our speech. Because we all rely on the music of our words to voice the emotionality of our speech, we all rely upon the intuitive potential of our right hemisphere. Yet, because we are all so overburdened with the need to master the logical aspects of life with our left hemisphere, we are victims of a wipe out effect. The irrational, instinctive, spontaneous emotional parts of ourselves get wiped out by the stringent and punctilious code of articulate logic. The effect is that we lose most of our innate musicality and bury the songful sonatas of the heart, retaining only that small vestige of melody which we need to bring prosody to our speech. Singing, which for the infant is the most natural form of expression, becomes charged and laden with fear and trepidation. Singing becomes something that we have to learn to do. Yet originally it was an instinct which we all possessed. Fortunately, however, instincts cannot be completely wiped out; they can only be driven underground.

Voice Movement Therapy involves uncovering the original instinct to sing and recalling the song of the soul. It is important for us to remember that the composition of song is a gift with which we were all blessed and one of the ways to retrieve it is to take the prosody of the spoken word and turn it back into melody, which is where it originates in the first place. For we sang out our feelings long before we spoke our thoughts.

Practical Method: Musicalising the Journey Song

Melody is merely exaggerated prosody, and because everybody uses prosody quite naturally, everyone has the potential ability to create melodies and make songs from their creative writing.

In this exercise, the client first reads the journey song in the same way as both the autobiography and the fairy tale have been read. Then the second time, the client listens carefully to the prosody underpinning the words: where the voice rises and where it falls in pitch; where the voice sustains and where it decays; where a string of syllables or words are uttered with notes in close proximity and where the voice moves across a broad pitch scale. Then, the client voices the journey song a third time, exaggerating this prosody and allowing it to turn into the outline of a melody. The fourth time, the client sings the journey song with a tune which has arisen organically from the prosody of the reading.

Client's Account: Vicky

Changing Tune

> The tune that emerged from the prosody of my lyrics reminded me of a nursery rhyme in that it was very simple and very rhythmic. The combination between the simple, innocent, child-like melody and the extremely non-innocent words put me in touch with the hideous relationship between an innocent child and sexual abuse; and it brought it home to me in a way that filled my singing with emotion. I felt like I was singing as both a child and an adult and my voice wavered between naïveté and bitterness. One moment I sounded like a baby and another like an old woman.

> As I sang, I recalled again how, when I was little, after an abusive episode, I would often sing quietly to myself after my father had left my room. I guess this was a kind of comforting. I was maybe mothering myself. Occasionally my mother would actually sing to me. In fact this was one of the few tender things I can remember her doing. And I remember that I loved it and would not want it to stop.

> Singing the song created the sense of encapsulating a set of images and memories in time, as though a number of things made sense on an emotional level: my mother's singing voice, my father's abusive attacks, my loneliness as a child, my spoiled innocence and my inhibited adult voice. Now I felt I wanted to sing the song with a different quality of voice. My voice sounded restricted and weak and I felt like I wanted to get angry but did not know how.

Client's Account: Richard

Something to Sing About

> In previous therapy I had grown tired of describing the accident time and time again from every angle. Every time I told it I hoped for some fresh light or some fresh relief. But mainly it seemed to just become cyclical. The story itself became a negative thing which threatened to loom over my head for evermore.

However, when it came to singing the song about the accident, I became so engaged in the act of singing and wanting to make something artistically valuable, that the personal origin of the song became secondary. The fact that it was my song and emanated from a crucial experience made me want to serve it well as a singer. But the fact that it was a song seemed to steer me away from a self-reflective exploration of its meaning towards a commitment to executing it with integrity and authenticity. I felt an incredible shift of sand and an amazing turn of the tables. The song about the accident became something to serve and embody and the singing made me feel good. In fact I had not enjoyed singing like this since before the accident when I was in a choir.

Also, the fact that others in the group seemed to be enjoying the song, as well as being emotionally moved by it, made me feel less like a poor victim worthy of sympathy and more like an able artist worthy of true engagement. What had been a personal tragedy that had inhibited my ability to communicate became, for a few moments, the thing that enabled me to be a communicative artist.

I felt like a singer with a tale to tell rather than a tale-teller whose tale prevented him from singing.

But, like Vicky, I felt dissatisfied with the sound of my voice because it did not seem to express the range of emotions that I felt underneath. I felt eager at this point to expand my voice in range and colour.

The Power of the Singing

Many great singers have endured life-long sufferings: they have been abused, beaten, degraded; they have lost loved ones in terrible accidents; they have fallen ill to eating disorders and disease; they have been imprisoned and enslaved. The truly great vocalist continues to sing in moments of the greatest and most personalised emotion. The singer makes her tragedies public by elevating them to the level of universal relevance. The song takes a personal event and an idiosyncratic image and turns it into an archetypal form. The singer suffers but her singing does not suffer as a result. Suffering may not be necessary in order to sing; but suffering is no reason not to sing – it is the best reason.

We cannot rewrite our history. The traumas which have befallen us in the past are etched upon our souls and no healing can rewrite history. But singing tricks history by succumbing to its immovable presence. Singing writes and rewrites the past. The song remains the same; it can be sung a million times by a million people. To sing about that which has disempowered us means that at some level we have overcome it.

But finding the tune or melody for a song is only the tip of the iceberg vocally and therapeutically. For the main therapeutic value in the use of the singing voice rests in the particular quality, colour or timbre of voice with which the tune is sung.

There are a thousand ways of singing the same melody for there are a thousand different qualities of voice with which a tune can be sung. And it is to a large extent the colour or quality or timbre of a voice which carries its emotional content. Therefore, once a client has discovered the means with which to create a melody from prosody, the next and most crucial step is to enable them to access a broad range of vocal qualities which in turn enable a song to be imbued with a diversity of emotion.

CHAPTER 5

The Ingredients of Voice
The Voice Movement Therapy System and the Musical Voice

The Ingredients of Voice

Every human voice is produced in the same way, yet every human voice is unique. The sound of a person's voice is like an acoustic fingerprint which carries their identity; and often our reactions to someone's voice are extremely subjective. Some voices attract us and others repel; some voices stimulate our agitation whilst others calm and soothe; some voices dominate with authority and others sound servile and sycophantic; some voices befriend and others contend; some voices we like and others we do not. Yet rarely do we take the time to consider exactly what it is in a certain voice that provokes our reactions. Without this understanding, we cannot really transcend our subjective judgements and gain insight into the psychology of vocal sound; and the best way to understand the voice is to break it down into the separate acoustic ingredients which combine to create vocal sound and learn how these ingredients are produced.

The human voice is made up of a set of ingredients which combine in different degrees to produce an infinite range of sounds, and there are ten basic ingredients which all voices possess. Our subjective reactions to voices are usually based on a response to these ingredients, just as our reactions to food are based on a response to the taste of specific ingredients which flavour the meal. By understanding the habitual recipe which makes up our own voice, we can make changes and choices, increasing the amount of one ingredient and decreasing the presence of another as we wish. Understanding the ingredients of the voice is therefore useful as a tool with which to analyse other voices and as a guide in the evolution of our own voice towards increasing malleability.

Each vocal ingredient also carries within it certain psychological implications. Just as we might choose to add or subtract specific herbs and spices to a recipe in order to create particular healing results, so the addition and subtraction of specific vocal ingredients can help to heal particular issues. However, in order to achieve this, we have to learn to access the ingredients, and this is made easier by the knowledge of how they are produced.

The ten ingredients of the voice according to the Voice Movement Therapy system are:

- Loudness
- Pitch
- Pitch fluctuation
- Register
- Harmonic timbre
- Nasality
- Free air
- Attack
- Disruption
- Articulation.

The following is a concise description of the nature of each ingredient and its main psychological pertinence.

Ingredient One: Loudness

Running from the lips to the lungs is a long elastic tube. This tube begins at the lips, opens out to become the mouth, curls downwards at the throat to become the pharynx which runs into the next section, known as the larynx, before turning into the trachea which, in the centre of the chest, splits into two tubes, one running into each lung. When we breathe in, air passes down this tube, inflating the lungs. When we breathe out, air passes up through this tube in the opposite direction, deflating the lungs. We shall call the part of this tube which extends from the lips to the larynx the voice tube (Figure 5.1).

Lying stretched out in the larynx are two flaps of tissue called the vocal cords. During normal breathing, the vocal cords lie at rest, one each side of the larynx, like an open pair of curtains allowing air to pass freely through a

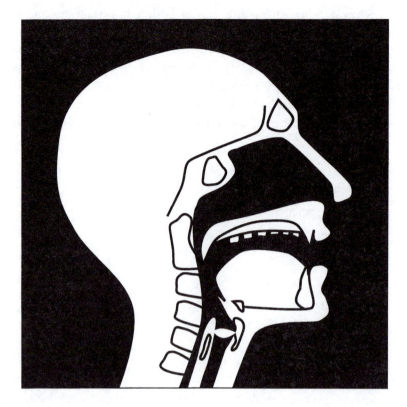

Figure 5.1

window. The window between the two vocal cords through which the air passes is called the glottis (Figure 5.2a). There are times, however, when we draw these vocal cords tightly shut, preventing air from passing through the tube in either direction. We often do this momentarily when lifting or moving a heavy object (Figure 5.2b).

The sound of the human voice is produced by the very rapid opening and closing of the vocal cords hundreds of times per second; this is often referred to as the vibration of the vocal cords. During this vibration the two vocal cords hit each other regularly like two hands clapping at great speed. When the vocal cords vibrate in this way they produce a note, just as a string gives off a note when it vibrates.

One of the things that causes the vocal cords to vibrate is the pressure of breath released from the lungs when we expire, just as the wind may cause a

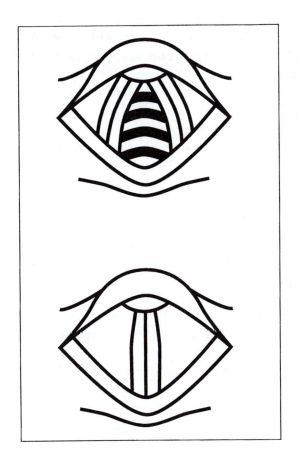

Figure 5.2

pair of curtains to flap and give off a sound at an open window. Because the vocal cords are opening and closing many times a second, the expired air is released in a series of infinitesimal puffs; and these puffs of air form a sound wave which carries the tone produced by the vocal cords through the voice tube and out through the mouth.

An increase in the pressure of breath travelling up from the lungs causes the vocal cords to vibrate with greater force, so that they hit each other harder. This produces a louder sound – just as an increase in the force and pressure of a wind would cause a pair of curtains to flap harder and more loudly at a window. To increase the pressure of the breath travelling up from the lungs through the voice tube, we have to contract the muscles of the chest and abdomen, squeezing the lungs empty with forceful pressure; and this increases the loudness of the voice by causing the vocal cords to hit into each other harder. To decrease the pressure of the breath, we have to ease off the force with which we contract the breathing muscles, squeezing the lungs more gently; and this decreases the loudness of the voice by causing the vocal cords to hit into each other more softly.

The first ingredient of the human voice is therefore loudness, which is perceived on a spectrum from loud to quiet.

Some Psychological Aspects of Loudness

The physical reasons which cause a person to have a loud or a quiet voice are connected to the use of the muscles which empty the lungs. But there are often psychological reasons why the muscles are employed in a particular way in the first place.

The quiet voice is often the sound of wisdom; and those with quiet voices may have reached a point where they do not need to make a loud noise, for they rest easily with their insight and are not driven to prove anything. The quiet voice is also equivalent to a soft touch; and some people maintain a voice which touches gently because that is how they wish to be touched. People with quiet voices may be emotionally bruised or sore; and in vocalising softly they may be asking for a tender voice in return to bandage the wounds of their heart. Many people who come into therapy and who find it difficult to produce a loud voice have been assaulted by the insensitive vocal loudness of their parents, partners or other individuals; and they are often frightened of producing a loud voice for fear of becoming like them. In many situations, extreme vocal loudness is associated with negative personality traits such as being 'loudmouthed', impudent, audacious, belligerent and pugnacious. In fact, sounds above 80 decibels are potentially destructive to physical tissue and mental processes. However, it can be a deeply healing experience to access very loud sounds and reclaim the positive side of extreme loudness. For the loud voice is also expressive of elation, excitement, joviality, rapture, rhapsody, celebration and delight; and these qualities can become obscured by an over-emphasis on the negative side to loudness. The loud voice is also one way that a person can fill space and claim their territory. The shadow side of this is that loudness also takes space away from others. Producing a loud voice is therefore often difficult for those who find it a struggle to claim their space and their right to a distinctive territory and platform from which to be heard.

There are many people who have no trouble with producing a loud voice and whose therapeutic process is more concerned with uncovering the voice of quietude. Whilst the loud voice halts a listener in their tracks, the quiet voice draws the listener in and is an invitation to intimacy and closeness. Many people develop loud and boisterous voices to mask a fear of such intimacy; and their healing journey often involves dissembling the defence around their vulnerability. Others have loud voices because they have had to shout in order to be heard above the crowd of a large family; and it is often difficult for them to have faith in the belief that they will find satisfaction even if they give voice to their needs quietly. Others have loud voices because they were constantly made to be quiet when they were young and have developed a booming voice as a way of defying this repression.

Like all ingredients, loudness has an almost infinite spectrum of potential psychological meanings which can only be understood accurately in the context of a compassionate and empathic relationship with each individual vocalist. However, the aforementioned ideas provide an impression of some of the more common psychological aspects of loudness.

Practical Method: Developing Loudness

To develop the loudness spectrum of the voice, clients stand comfortably and breathe in and out through the mouth. They then begin to vocalise on a note in the middle of their pitch range and then begin ascending and descending in steps and slides. As they do this, they decrease the loudness of the voice until they are vocalising as quietly as possible. Then, as they ascend and descend in pitch, they increase the loudness by degrees until they are vocalising as loudly as possible. Thinking of having a spectrum of loudness from very quiet to extremely loud, clients take time to vocalise between these two extremes covering all the shades between. Finally, it is useful for them to take a simple song and sing it three times: once very quietly, once with moderate loudness and once as loud as they can.

Ingredient Two: Pitch

The faster any object vibrates, the higher the note it produces. So the faster the vocal cords vibrate, the higher the pitch of the human voice. To sing the lowest C on the piano, the vocal cords would have to vibrate 32 times per second; to sing the highest C on the piano, the vocal cords would have to vibrate 4186 times per second.

If we wanted to produce a higher note from a vibrating string we would have to tighten it, whilst to lower the note we would have to slacken the string. The same principle applies to the vocal cords. If we tighten and stretch the cords they vibrate at a faster rate and produce a higher pitch; if we slacken them they vibrate more slowly and produce a lower pitch. But the thicker a string is, the more you have to tighten it to produce a high note. This is why the thin strings on a guitar do not have to be tightened as much as the thick strings to produce the same pitch. The same principle applies to the human voice; and because men have thicker vocal cords than women, they have to tighten them more to achieve high notes. Conversely, it is more difficult for women to produce low notes because their vocal cords are thinner. However, the majority of factors which prevent men from singing high and women from singing low are psychological and can be overcome.

The space between two notes is called an interval; and it is the memory of the intervals between notes rather than the notes themselves which enable us to recall a song. When we sing 'Happy Birthday', we can recall the melody because we know the intervals; but the notes themselves are not fixed – we can start the song on any pitch so long as the intervals between all the following notes are correct.

Given that pitch is made up of vibratory frequency, the human voice can obviously sing a vast spectrum of notes by changing the speed of vocal cord vibration. But the European classical western scale only classes certain frequencies as proper notes. This scale divides the potential range of frequencies into an octave of notes which we can play on the piano. But there are other notes which exist between the keys on the piano which the voice can sing even though there is no string and no hammer for that vibratory frequency on the piano.

Different cultures divide the potential pitch range in different ways. For example, whilst western music has an octave of eight notes, classical Indian music has a scale of 22 notes. What is regarded as a musical note in one place is regarded as redundant in another. But in talking rather than singing, people from all cultures are free from aligning the pitch range of their voice with a set scale and the voice rises and falls through the complete range of potential frequencies. This is why singing traditions that originate in the fields and along the railway tracks – where people extend their natural speaking voices into a call – do not suffer from the restrictions of formal music.

The second ingredient of the human voice is therefore pitch, also referred to as 'note', which is perceived on a spectrum from low to high.

Some Psychological Aspects of Pitch

The height and depth of a voice is dependent upon the vibratory speed of the vocal cords, which is in turn dependent on their thickness and the tension of the muscles which tighten and slacken them. But everybody has the capacity to cover an extremely wide pitch range; and the reasons why a person has a particularly high or low voice are primarily psychological.

We tend to raise the pitch of the voice in joy and excitement and people with habitually high voices may seek to reside in the realm of pleasure. But the high voice may also serve as a way of avoiding the sorrowful and sombre emotions associated with the deeps.

Like sounds above a certain loudness threshold, sounds produced by extremely high frequencies can be penetrating and destructive. High sounds are usually sensed as being sharp and can be experienced as piercing objects. Some people may develop high voices in order to feel that they have the power to penetrate obstacles, cut through the opposition and forge the way ahead. Other people have extreme difficulty in accessing the high voice because the sense of power which the high voice evokes causes feelings of shame. For those who suffer from a depleted sense of self-worth, accessing the high voice can be extremely empowering. Reaching the high voice can feel as though we have reached new personal heights and achieved a heightened sense of awareness.

High sounds are experienced as being high in space and, during a therapeutic process, the vocalist will often reach up with the body when singing high in Pitch, as though plucking notes from the air. High sounds instigate feelings of elation and flightiness and for those people who seek to relieve themselves from the depressive monotony of the earth, making high sounds can be extremely liberating. But for those whose tendency is to be ungrounded and unearthed, high sounds can be disorientating and unsettling.

At the other end of the pitch scale is the low voice, which in opera is called bass. This 'bass' voice often expresses the 'base' aspects of our soul which has two dimensions. First, our base is our bedrock, our foundations and the ground upon which our character stands. To access the low voice therefore gives us a sense of deep-rootedness, strength and support. But base also means crude, unrefined, flagrant, obscene and coarse; and vocalising with the low voice enables us to express a certain primeval core of sensation. For those whose healing requires a redeeming of animal instincts and primal passions, the low voice can be very liberating. The low voice feels as though it emerges from deep in the body and making bass sounds can stimulate the sexual organs and stir erotic energy. Many people avoid low sounds as a way of evading their sexuality.

The deep voice is experienced as being low in space and when we vocalise with a bass voice it feels as if we are descending into the deeps physically and emotionally. The low voice can cause us to feel down in the dumps, in the pits, in the doldrums and depressed. Many people have deep voices because their soul resides in the depths of depression, whilst others avoid low sounds so they do not have to confront the morose and depressive aspects of themselves. Our voice descends in sorrow and rises in joy; and many people develop low voices because they have become overwhelmed with sorrow and forgotten the magic of joy.

The low voice sounds as though it emerges from the depths and is therefore associated with depth of integrity, depth of meaning and authority. The high voice can therefore be misread as superficial and lacking in psychological depth. Some people develop low voices in order to preserve a sense of psychological depth whilst others may develop high voices in order to avoid the responsibility which comes with speaking from the deeps.

Like all ingredients, Pitch has an almost infinite spectrum of potential psychological meanings which can only be understood accurately in the context of a compassionate and empathic relationship with each individual vocalist. However, the aforementioned ideas provide an impression of some of the more common psychological aspects of pitch.

Practical Method: Developing Pitch

Having explored the spectrum of loudness, clients return to a note in the middle of their pitch range and begin ascending and descending in pitch with moderate loudness. When they reach what feels like the top of their pitch range, they try adjusting the loudness to see if this helps them to go higher than they have before. They do the same thing when they reach what feels like the bottom of the pitch range. When they have found the level of loudness which enables them to extend the ends of the pitch range, they practise going a little higher and a little lower than they would normally so that in time they extend the range of pitches accessible.

Ingredient Three: Pitch Fluctuation

When we vocalise, the speed with which the vocal folds vibrate does not remain constant but wavers to some degree. Even if we attempt to sing a single note for a prolonged period of time, for example middle C, the vocal folds will not sustain their opening and closing at an exact and constant 256 times per second. There will be some fluctuation as the vocal cords vibrate a little faster and a little slower in a given unit of time. In western singing, if the fluctuation is too great, for example fluctuating between 236 and 276 times per second, then the note will sound wobbly and the voice will be judged to be out of tune, particularly if the fluctuation is very slow. But if the fluctuation is minimal – for example between 246 and 266 times per second – and the fluctuation occurs very quickly, then the note will have a quality known as vibrato and the voice will be judged to be classically beautiful. Yet both the revered vibrato and the despised wavering are produced by the same effect. This effect is called pitch fluctuation.

In many indigenous forms of singing the voice is free to fluctuate spontaneously without falling prey to extreme judgments regarding its musical viability. Many of these singing styles originate in the extension of the speaking voice and capitalise on the fact that the speaking voice fluctuates freely in people from all cultures without regard to musical correctness. To draw upon the healing power of the voice we have to suspend our western judgements and allow the voice to fluctuate freely, just as the psyche fluctuates in its wheel of passions.

The third ingredient of the human voice is therefore pitch fluctuation, which is perceived as being fast or slow, great or small.

Some Psychological Aspects of Pitch Fluctuation

In daily life, pitch fluctuation occurs to our voice when we are extremely anxious or nervous; and often the quivering can tingle through the muscles of our whole body. Vocalising with pitch fluctuation can instil feelings of uncertainty, creating the sensation of having an insecure and unstable personality; and those who have a lot of pitch fluctuation in their voice are often of a nervous and insecure disposition. For those whose therapeutic process is concerned with replacing such an unassured persona with confidence and ease, substituting pitch fluctuation with constant tones is extremely assuring. On the other hand, those whose voices lack pitch fluctuation may be holding fast to their security and avoiding the vulnerable and uncertain parts of themselves. For those whose healing requires old patterns to be shaken up and fixed habits to be dislodged, vocalising with pitch fluctuation can provide the earthquake out of which fresh perspectives can grow.

Pitch fluctuation often occurs when we are excited and for those who have lost the elated and tumultuous part of the soul, vocalising with pitch fluctuation can serve to arouse the spirit. But pitch fluctuation also occurs when we are afraid; and vocalising with pitch fluctuation can evoke feelings of panic and fright. For those whose lives are limited by fear, it is extremely healing to replace pitch fluctuation with constant notes. But for those who want to taste fear again in order to reclaim the sense of forces greater than themselves, vocalising with pitch fluctuation can serve to unnerve the complacent spirit and fill the soul with awe and respect for the unknown.

Like all ingredients, pitch fluctuation has an almost infinite spectrum of potential psychological meanings which can only be understood accurately in the context of a compassionate and empathic relationship with each individual vocalist. However, the aforementioned ideas provide an impression of some of the more common psychological aspects of pitch fluctuation.

Practical Method: Developing Pitch Fluctuation

Now clients have a wide pitch range which they sing with varying degrees of loudness, they try to vocalise this range with pitch fluctuation. First, they sing their pitch range with a very fast fluctuation, like a classical vibrato. Then they sing the range again with a slower pitch fluctuation. As they do this, they vary the level of loudness and continue seeking to go higher and lower than they have before, allowing themselves to celebrate having three vocal ingredients to play with.

Ingredient Four: Register

If you sing the lowest note in your pitch range and rise one note at a time up to the highest, you will notice that somewhere in the middle there is a transitional point where a particular change occurs to the quality of the voice. The upper notes will probably seem to have a brighter quality whilst the lower notes will sound darker. The point where this change occurs is called the register break. The two main registers are modal and falsetto. The lower range of notes which sound darker are in modal register and the upper range of notes which sound brighter are in falsetto register. In the western classical tradition, a female falsetto voice is called 'head register' and her modal voice is called 'chest register'. These terms originate in the antiquated idea that falsetto register generates more vibration in the head whilst the modal register resonates more in the chest; but there is no scientific evidence for this. The term 'falsetto' comes from the Latin for 'false' and calling this quality of voice 'falsetto register' in a male voice and 'head register' in a female voice implies that it is false for a man but not for a woman to sing with this quality. Indeed, the association between falsetto and femininity is exaggerated in the pastiche cabaret and pantomime when men use the falsetto register to impersonate the speaking voice of a woman. This is of course unfounded because neither women nor men speak in falsetto, but in modal. But both men and women do use falsetto in their talking voice at times of extreme emotion, such as when we sob or laugh.

In opera, singers are prohibited from exposing the change of register and each singer must use one or the other. The male voices are always sung in modal – with the exception of the male counter tenor – whilst falsetto is reserved for women. But outside of European classical music, in western contemporary singing and non-western indigenous styles, both registers are used freely by men and women and are not associated with masculinity or femininity. The Register break is particularly exaggerated in the yodelling style of singing often associated with the indigenous music of the Swiss Alps and amongst the North American 'singing cowboys' such as Jimmie Rodgers, Eddy Arnold and Tennessee Ernie Ford. Some of these men sing from the range of an operatic bass up to the heights associated with the soprano. Elvis Presley and Roy Orbison also moved fluidly between modal and falsetto. There have also been a number of contemporary western male singers who sing exclusively in the falsetto register, such as the Bee Gees and Jimmy Somerville; and there are female singers who make a point of singing exclusively in modal.

Although the higher pitch range of a voice is usually sung in falsetto and the lower pitch range in modal, register is not directly related to pitch because with practice you can sing a range of notes in modal and then sing the same range of notes again in falsetto.

Because the deliberate exposure of the register break is not allowed in opera, trainees of classical singing learn a technique called blending. This involves ascending and descending the pitch range, gradually blending the qualities of falsetto and modal into a single quality known as a 'blended' register so that the break is eradicated. However, this also eradicates the special emotional magnetism of the register break. To reclaim the full power of the voice, it is necessary to develop both the modal and falsetto registers and allow the voice to move between the two as the mood requires.

The fourth ingredient of the voice is therefore register which is perceived as being either modal, falsetto or blended.

Some Psychological Aspects of Register

A common term for a change in register is a 'break' and indeed as the voice passes from modal to falsetto or vice versa it can feel as though something is breaking. Some people have a constant register break in their daily voice; and often this reveals a deep part of the Self which has been broken and has not healed. Our voice breaks naturally when we are breaking down with emotion; and deep crying is often characterised by a sobbing back and forth between the two registers. But the same register break often occurs when we laugh fully and without restraint. Some people never allow the registers to change, even when they laugh or cry, as a way of avoiding contact with genuine emotion. For those people whose therapeutic journey is concerned with finding access to tumultuous emotions and reactivating the passions of the heart, the register break can be extremely liberating. On the other hand, for those who experience a constant 'breaking' of emotion, replacing the register break with a blended constant quality can be very stabilising and strengthening.

Because, in the west, falsetto is associated more with femininity and modal with masculinity, the vocal Registers have a healing power when it comes to sexuality. When a man accesses pure falsetto and a woman accesses pure modal, sexual stereotypes can be overcome and a more holistic sense of gender can be invigorated.

Because the falsetto register is the quality which characterises a child's voice, accessing the falsetto can animate the inner child; and for those who have lost the spirit of youth, this can be very healing. Conversely, for those whose lives are under the constant spell of regression and whose healing journey seeks an opportunity to mature, the modal voice can be very grounding.

Using the healing voice means allowing the voice to break out of one register into another so that we may break out of the fixity of a rigid Self and express our capacity for change and growth.

Like all ingredients, register has an almost infinite spectrum of potential psychological meanings which can only be understood accurately in the context of a compassionate and empathic relationship with each individual vocalist. However, the aforementioned ideas provide an impression of some of the more common psychological aspects of register.

Practical Method: Developing Register

Clients start singing at the bottom of their pitch range and ascend one note at a time, listening for the two notes where the voice changes from modal to falsetto register. They then refind those notes and sing them over and over, vocalising on a yodel. Then, having acquired the art of the register break, they practise yodelling in other parts of the pitch range, allowing the voice to create improvised melodies which use modal and falsetto. Finally, they sing a range of notes in modal and then practise singing the same range of notes in falsetto.

Ingredient Five: Harmonic Timbre

The section of the voice tube which runs from the lips to the larynx can change its length and its diameter; and because of the laws of acoustics, the same note produced by the vibration of the vocal cords will resonate with a very different quality if the voice tube is short and narrow to the quality produced when the voice tube is lengthened and dilated.

To understand this, imagine three basic tubes, closed at the bottom but open at the top, constructed with different diameters and different lengths. The first is short and narrow; the second is relatively longer and wider; and the third is much longer and more dilated again. Imagine that we hold a tuning fork vibrating at 256 times per second – which produces middle C – over the top of each tube in turn and listen to the sound of the note echoing or resonating inside the tubes. In moving from listening to the sound inside the first tube to the same note echoing or resonating in the second and then the third, we would hear a change of timbre. Perhaps the sound in the first tube would sound 'bright', 'twangy', 'shiny' and 'shimmery'; perhaps the sound resonating in the second tube, by comparison, would sound 'thicker', more 'solemn' or 'fruitier'; and perhaps the sound resonating in the third tube

Figure 5.3

would sound 'full', 'moaning', 'rounded' and 'dark'. Probably, the first tube would sound more comparable to a flute, the second tube would sound more comparable to the clarinet, whilst the sound produced by the third tube would sound more akin to the saxophone; they would all however produce the note C.

With regard to voice production, both the length and the diameter of the voice tube can alter. The diameter of the voice tube can increase by opening the mouth and stretching the throat; and the length of the voice tube can increase by lowering the larynx in the neck. The tube can therefore assume three different configurations comparable to the three shapes of the three crude tubes (Figure 5.3). The first is called Flute Configuration, whereby the larynx is high in the neck and the tube is quite narrow, such as when we blow a kiss or whistle (Figure 5.4). The second is called Clarinet Configuration, whereby the larynx is positioned in the middle of the neck and the tube is more dilated, such as when we steam up a pair of glasses (Figure 5.5). The third is called Saxophone Configuration, whereby the larynx is fully descended in the neck and the tube is dilated to its maximum, such as when we yawn (Figure 5.6).

If the vibration of the vocal cords is maintained at a constant vibratory frequency, say at 256 times per second, producing middle C, whilst the vocal tract moves from Flute Configuration through Clarinet Configuration to Saxophone Configuration, the effect will be to sing the same note with three very distinct timbres, comparable to that achieved when playing the note C

Figure 5.4   Figure 5.5

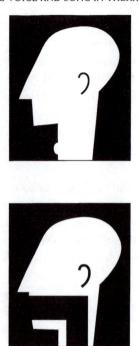

Figure 5.6

on a tuning fork held above the three separate crude tubes imagined earlier. In Voice Movement Therapy, we give the vocal colour produced by a short narrow voice tube the instrumental name Flute Timbre; we name the vocal colour produced by a medium length and diameter tube Clarinet Timbre; and we call the vocal colour produced by a fully lengthened and dilated voice tube Saxophone Timbre.

The fifth ingredient of the human voice is therefore harmonic timbre which can be Flute, Clarinet or Saxophone, depending on the configuration of the voice tube.

Some Psychological Aspects of Harmonic Timbre

The breath emerging from the tube when it is in Flute Configuration is cold – it is the shape we make with our mouth when we want to cool down hot food by blowing air from the mouth. The sound of the Flute Timbre can also feel cool, passionless, stoic and frosty. Furthermore, because the Flute Configuration tube is so narrow, it does not discharge a great deal of acoustic or emotional material and it can sound very reserved and conservative. For those whose therapeutic journey is directed towards learning to preserve more energy and more privacy, such as those who have been depleted and exhausted by their tendency to give too much of themselves, vocalising in Flute Timbre can be very helpful. But for those seeking to release more of their Self into the world, it is necessary to expand the dimensions of the voice tube. In singing, the Flute Timbre is heard at its most constant in Christian plainsong, such as the Gregorian Chant.

Whilst the Flute Configuration tends to release a minimum amount of breath and sound, the Saxophone Configuration releases the entire flood and holds very little back. For those who are seeking to release themselves from the stifling confines of a reserved and retained psyche, vocalising in Saxophone Timbre can be extremely transforming. Common reasons for expanding the throat to the dimensions of the Saxophone Configuration are to belch or vomit. Therefore, vocalising with the Saxophone Timbre can feel as though we are going to bring things up from the stomach. It is, in fact, very rare for someone actually to vomit when vocalising in Saxophone Timbre; however, it is common for people initially to experience the Saxophone Timbre as 'sick' and ugly. Although this can be terrifying, it is also very liberating for those whose healing is connected to being released from the pressure of having to be beautiful, sweet and correct.

Expanding the voice tube also often raises issues connected to sexuality, for the more open the tube becomes, the more likely it feels that one may be penetrated. In addition, as the tube expands and lengthens, it can feel as if the voice is emerging from the pelvic area and animating a libidinous drive.

Another reason for expanding the voice tube dimensions to the maximum is to cry; and vocalising with the Saxophone Timbre often induces sobbing, which can be very liberating for those who have become separated from their sorrows. On the other hand, for those who seek to be healed from feeling overwhelmed with the water of their sadness, it is helpful to narrow the voice tube to Clarinet Configuration or Flute Configuration. In singing, the Saxophone Timbre is often heard in Gospel and jazz; Cleo Laine and Nina Simone, for example, both use fully expanded voice tube configurations.

Between Flute and Saxophone is the Clarinet Timbre, which is emblematic of the middle ground. It can narrow to Flute or it can expand to Saxophone. For those seeking to increase their choices and dexterity, the Clarinet Configuration is a grail worth pursuing, for it is a platform from which all else is possible.

In Voice Movement Therapy, being able to expand the voice tube dimensions is the single most important part of the physical work. For the expanded tube enables all the other vocal ingredients to be reverberated, amplified and enhanced. Expanding the tube therefore enables people to make the most of themselves, to reveal themselves in all their colours. However, dealing with all the psychological inhibitions which prevent the tube from expanding and the soul from being amplified constitutes one of the most important areas of psychological work. Expanding the tube means expanding the Self; thus it sits at the core of the healing process.

Like all ingredients, harmonic timbre has an almost infinite spectrum of potential psychological meanings which can only be understood accurately in the context of a compassionate and empathic relationship with each individual vocalist. However, the aforementioned ideas provide an impression of some of the more common psychological aspects of harmonic timbre. I have described at length the physicality and psychology of this process in the first volume of this series, *Using Voice and Movement in Therapy: The Practical Application of Voice Movement Therapy* (Newham 1999).

Practical Method: Developing Harmonic Timbre

Clients stand comfortably and breathe in and out through the mouth. They then narrow the voice tube to Flute Configuration by whistling or blowing cool air as though to lower the temperature of hot food. It is useful for clients to imagine that the voice tube is very narrow and that it extends from the lips down to the indent between the clavicles at the top of the breast bone. They now begin to vocalise, singing up and down the pitch range with varying degrees of loudness in modal and falsetto register, listening to the Flute Timbre of the voice.

They now expand the dimensions of the voice tube to Clarinet Configuration, opening the mouth and expanding the throat. It is useful for them to imagine that they are steaming up a window or a pair of spectacles and to feel how the expired breath is now warm. Clients now imagine that the tube is wider and that it extends from the lips down to the centre of the torso at the bottom of the breast bone. They then begin to vocalise, singing up and down the pitch range with varying degrees of loudness in modal and falsetto register, listening to the Clarinet Timbre of the voice.

They then expand the voice tube to its maximum dimensions, dilating mouth and throat as though yawning and imagine that the tube extends from the lips all the way down into the belly. Clients then begin to vocalise, singing up and down the pitch range with varying degrees of loudness in modal and falsetto register, listening to the Saxophone Timbre of the voice.

Now, they take a melody and sing it first in Flute Timbre then in Clarinet Timbre and then in Saxophone Timbre but keep all the other vocal ingredients constant so that they can hear specifically the three distinct harmonic timbres.

Ingredient Six: Nasality

As the air carries the sound up from the larynx, not all of it passes through the mouth and exits at the lips; some also passes up above the roof of the mouth and through the nasal passages, exiting at the nose. Sound which passes through this tube resonates with a quality which is usually referred to as nasal. In Voice Movement Therapy, we give this nasal quality the instrumental name 'Violin' which combines with the Flute, Clarinet or Saxophone Timbre of the voice.

The more air that passes through the nasal passages, the more nasality or Violin the sound of the voice will have; and the quantity of air passing through the passages is controlled by a flap of tissue known as the soft palate. This trap door hangs at the back of the throat and can open and close by degrees. If it is completely closed, then the voice has no Violin and sounds lacking in all nasality. If it is completely open, then the voice has a lot of Violin and sounds very nasal. Between these two extremes a whole spectrum is possible, like adding or subtracting violins from the string section of an orchestra.

Violin is the quality of voice that children use when they impersonate a Chinese or Japanese person; and though this is a social stereotype, nasality is in fact a tonal colour inherent in a lot of indigenous oriental singing and can be heard in the voices of the Cantonese Opera, the Shanghai Opera and those of the Hát Chéo Folk Theatre of Vietnam. There have also been a number of western contemporary singers whose voices are infused with a lot of Violin, such as Billie Holiday, Marlene Dietrich, Neil Young and Bob Dylan in his early work.

The sixth ingredient of the voice is therefore nasality or Violin which is perceived on a spectrum from minimum to maximum.

Some Psychological Aspects of Nasality

Violin is the quality of voice which people automatically use when impersonating a baby or a very old person. Violin therefore carries with it issues connected to age. People who complain that their voices are too child-like usually have a lot of Violin in their voice and by learning to decrease nasal resonance they can experience a new self-image, replacing naïveté with maturity.

It is very common for actors to use nasality when playing someone wicked and it is our natural tendency to use Violin when we are expressing spite and vindictiveness. For those seeking to get in touch with their malice and animosity, vocalising with Violin can be very provocative.

Nasality is used a lot more in the speaking voice than in most western singing styles. In fact, there are certain vowels in the English language, such as 'i' as in 'sit', which cannot be adequately communicated without increasing nasality – which is why they are called 'nasal vowels'. In indigenous cultures where the singing style has evolved from speaking and calling, there is often a lot more Violin in the voices. Accessing Violin is therefore a key to sonically empathising with the voices of other lands and can help us get in touch with our multi-cultural and transpersonal self.

Acoustically, Violin brings to the voice a certain hardness and density, enabling the voice to be projected over greater distances and to be heard above other noise. This is another reason why indigenous singing styles which have originated in the open air and where people had to sing to each other over large distances tend to have a lot of Violin in the voices. For those who wish to acquire the ability to project their voice, vocalising with Violin is extremely supportive and brings strength and solidity to the sound.

Like all ingredients, Violin has an almost infinite spectrum of potential psychological meanings which can only be understood accurately in the context of a compassionate and empathic relationship with each individual vocalist. However, the aforementioned ideas provide an impression of some of the more common psychological aspects of Violin.

Practical Method: Developing Nasality

Clients take a note in the middle of their Pitch range and sing it with moderate loudness without pitch fluctuation in modal register and Clarinet Timbre. Now, as they sing the note, they add Violin by making the sound more nasal. They then practise singing this note with a spectrum of Violin from minimum to maximum.

Clients now sing another note with moderate loudness, without pitch fluctuation and in Clarinet Timbre but in falsetto register and again practise increasing and decreasing the amount of Violin.

When they have acquired control of nasality, they can begin experimenting with different combinations of the other vocal ingredients as they play with the addition and subtraction of Violin.

Ingredient Seven: Free Air

When the vocal cords vibrate, they push together momentarily many times per second. But if, during their moment of contact, they do not push tightly together, then breath seeps through the crack. When this happens, the sound of the voice is very breathy. In Voice Movement Therapy such a breathy quality in the tonal colour of a voice is called Free Air. The more loosely the vocal cords push together, the more Free Air the voice will have.

During the 1950s, Julie London elevated the Free Air voice to new heights with her rendition of 'Cry Me a River'; and there are a number of singers in more recent western contemporary music whose voices have a lot of Free Air, such as Art Garfunkel.

The seventh ingredient of the human voice is therefore Free Air which is generally referred to as the 'breathiness' of a voice and is perceived on a spectrum from minimum to maximum.

Some Psychological Aspects of Free Air

Increasing Free Air is something which many people do when expressing empathy, gentility and receptivity, whilst voices without any Free Air usually sound firm. For those people seeking to melt their hard exterior and access their underlying sensitivity, vocalising with maximum Free Air is ideal. But for those who tend to leave themselves without guard and protection, vocalising with minimum Free Air can create a greater sense of strength and resilience.

A voice rich in Free Air is often associated with sexuality; and sexuality is always latently present in the act of singing. The art of singing is, in essence, founded upon the ability to stimulate and arouse the listener with the sensuous use of the mouth. Some singers have exaggerated the sensual aspect to singing and often use Free Air to eroticise the tonal colour of their voice. Marilyn Monroe was probably the first to epitomise this style. For those seeking to uncover their buried sexuality, vocalising with Free Air can be extremely liberating, unleashing the libido in sound.

We also tend to fill the voice with Free Air when we are exasperated and perplexed; and vocalising with Free Air can tap into these feelings.

Vocalising with Free Air is exhausting because the sound absorbs so much breath that you have to replenish the air in the lungs frequently, only to lose it all again in the next sound. This can create a feeling of futility and of 'not getting anywhere'. For such people, as well for those who feel that they lack reserves and who need to lessen their tendency to over-expend, decreasing the amount of Free Air can be very healing. But for those who feel the tension and pressure of keeping their spirit contained, increasing the amount of Free Air in the voice can feel extremely releasing.

Like all ingredients, Free Air has an almost infinite spectrum of potential psychological meanings which can only be understood accurately in the context of a compassionate and empathic relationship with each individual vocalist. However, the aforementioned ideas provide an impression of some of the more common psychological aspects of Free Air.

Practical Method: Developing Free Air

Clients sing an improvised melody in a voice with moderate loudness. They now repeat the singing but this time they sing it as though they are vocalising on a whisper. As they sing, clients make the sound as breathy as they can, filling the voice with Free Air. Now, they decrease the amount of Free Air so that the voice is moderately breathy. Finally, they remove the Free Air completely and sing with a voice that is firm and solid. Finally, they practise combining varying amounts of Free Air with all the other vocal ingredients.

Ingredient Eight: Attack

The pressure of the breath travelling up from the lungs determines the force with which the vocal cords contact each other during vibration which in turn determines the loudness of the voice. However, the vocal cords also have the capacity to hit into each other under the power of their own neuromuscular connections. This means that they can increase or decrease the force of contact. This extra dimension to vocal fold vibration is called attack. Increased attack does not make the voice louder but gives it a certain stress.

The eighth ingredient of the human voice is therefore attack which gives a voice its stress and is perceived on a spectrum from lesser to greater.

Some Psychological Aspects of Attack

Vocal attack is used when we want to attack our subject with a strength of opinion and certainty and those whose voices are naturally abundant with this quality are often quite strong-minded and strong-willed individuals. We often use increased attack when we are driving our point home with the punctilious and percussive points of our argument. Vocal attack is often used when we are certain of ourselves and those people with a lot of attack in their voices are often those with a sense of self-esteem and sometimes self-righteousness. For those people who have succumbed to this mask at the expense of their vulnerable and uncertain self, decreasing attack can uncover a tone of greater humility.

Those whose voices lack attack are often dealing with reticence and self-doubt, lacking the necessary belief in themselves with which to attack the world with their voice. For those with a tendency to acquiesce and relinquish their beliefs when intimidated or opposed, vocalising with attack can help to muster a new adversarial spirit and consolidate the ability to hold ground.

Because attack tends to create a percussive dimension, people who naturally use this quality are usually those who think in a linear direction and feel at ease with logic and lists of reasons for and against the decision at hand. Those who lack this quality in their voice, on the other hand, are generally those more at ease with non-linear intuitive thought which meanders and explores issues elliptically. Attack is the rhythmic component to the voice and, for those whose expressions are full of flow but who have lost a sense of tempo in their lives, vocalising with attack can be very grounding. On the other hand, those who have been sequestered by the overbearing demands of time can experience a healing liberation by replacing attack with the soft edges of a gentle tonal colour in their voice.

Like all ingredients, attack has an almost infinite spectrum of potential psychological meanings which can only be understood accurately in the context of a compassionate and empathic relationship with each individual vocalist. However, the aforementioned ideas provide an impression of some of the more common psychological aspects of attack.

Practical Method: Developing Attack

To develop increased attack, clients take a series of vowels preceded by an 'H' and say them quickly and percussively on the expired breath as though they are releasing a series of bullets: Ha, Hi, Ho, He. Then, they sustain the strength of the attack through an extended note on these sounds: Haaaaaaaa, Hiiiiiiii, Hoooooooo, Heeeeeeee.

Ingredient Nine: Disruption

Sometimes, the two vocal cords do not meet so as to create a flush, smooth edge but instead crash together unevenly with corrugated edges, rubbing into each other and creating friction. When this happens the tonal colour of the voice becomes rough and the pitch becomes discontinuous. In Voice Movement Therapy such a voice is described as possessing disruption. Disrupted sounds also arise when other tissue structures of the larynx vibrate or come into contact with the vocal cords.

Disruption is a key component of many non-western indigenous singing styles, such as the chanting of Tibetan monks and the rough calling of Flamenco Deep Song. However, singers of these traditions have great difficulty in producing any other kind of non-disrupted sound because constant friction between the vocal cords causes damage to their constituting tissue. There are also many people in the tradition of western contemporary music who have used disruption, such as Janis Joplin, Louis Armstrong, Rod Stewart, Tom Waits, Bonnie Tyler and Tina Turner; and some of these people have also suffered vocal damage. There are however ways of producing a disrupted voice which protect the cords from damage, but these techniques need to be learned from someone first hand.

The ninth ingredient of the human voice is therefore disruption and is perceived on a spectrum from mild to severe.

Some Psychological Aspects of Disruption

We tend to use disruption when we are extremely angry and when we are scolding someone with a warning; and those with naturally disrupted voices are often host to a backlog of rage. However, the voice also disrupts when we are emotionally disrupted and many people with such voices have been shattered by intense and overwhelming experiences. Conversely, those people who have difficulty vocalising with disruption are often avoiding both their anger and the broken, disrupted and shattered part of themselves. People who cannot access their disrupted voices tend to be stoic and highly attached to the idea of themselves as able and well balanced. For such people, the sound of disruption is too extreme and too threatening, for it promises to overturn the polished persona by sprinkling grit across the smooth surface of the vocal mask. For those seeking to unearth their anger or disturb the perfect grace of their clean-cut person, accessing disruption can be radically transformative.

Like all ingredients, disruption has an almost infinite spectrum of potential psychological meanings which can only be understood accurately in the context of a compassionate and empathic relationship with each individual vocalist. However, the aforementioned ideas provide an impression of some of the more common psychological aspects of disruption.

Practical Method: Developing Disruption

Clients should not practise disruption for longer than a few minutes unless the practitioner is certain that they have been taught a way of creating disrupting sounds which do not threaten the health and longevity of the vocal instrument. As with all of the methods described in this chapter, the practitioner should have mastered the vocal techniques before attempting to impart them to clients. The safest way to get a sense of disruption is to vocalise very quietly in the middle of the pitch range in modal register with very little attack and in Saxophone Timbre.

Clients begin vocalising on a single note and then start to groan gently as though simmering with fury. As the voice becomes disrupted, they travel up and down the lower part of the pitch range and improvise a melody.

Ingredient Ten: Articulation

When we are babies we use the complete palette of articulate shapes available to us as we sculpture vocal sounds with the lips, jaw and tongue. But when we learn the mother tongue we abandon this range for the narrow spectrum of our spoken language. Only in extreme circumstances, such as speaking in tongues during spiritual ritual or speaking in psychic disarray during mental illness, do we reclaim this spectrum of articulation.

The two units of articulation which are present in all tongues are vowels and consonants. Vowels are open sounds made from a continuous air flow. Consonants are plosive sounds made by interrupting the air flow. In Voice Movement Therapy, articulation does not refer just to the vowels and consonants of a single recognisable linguistic code; it refers to the complete range of articulated structures which can be created by the human vocal instrument. To reclaim the healing power of the voice means returning to the complete palette of sculptured sounds – in effect it means singing in all tongues.

The tenth ingredient of the human voice is therefore articulation which is the sculpturing of the vocal sound into vowels and consonants with mouth, lips, tongue and jaw.

Some Psychological Aspects of Articulation

In the early stages of accessing the complete range of the voice, any form of articulation can be restricting, causing the throat to tighten and the voice tube to narrow in preparation for words. But, articulation is also a very liberating ingredient of the human voice because it provides a sense of giving a precise shape to the feeling carried by the voice. For those who find the spoken language of their mother tongue an unfriendly means of communication, singing in a multitude of spontaneous tongues provides a deep level of psychological release as though a new and perfect language has been uncovered.

Practical Method: Developing Articulation

Clients begin by calling out a long note. They let the voice ascend and descend in pitch and allow the ingredients of the voice to combine spontaneously. Then, they begin to vocalise familiar articulate word units: Ta, Go, Sha, Be. As they call out, they start to allow themselves to give shape to word units which are less familiar: Ach, Unf, Tfi, Yin. It is useful for them to imagine that they are touring the world's languages, singing excerpts from every tongue that ever was. As they sing, they imagine that they are touring the Occident and Orient, the northern and the southern hemispheres of the globe and giving voice to the lands which they discover.

The Complete Palette

These ten ingredients make up the palette of tonal colours which can be heard woven into the fabric of every human voice; and I have provided a comprehensive demonstration of all the vocal ingredients in the singing and speaking voice on a complete audio course *The Singing Cure* (Newham 1998). To recap, the ten ingredients which make up the human voice are:

Ingredient One: Loudness, perceived on a spectrum from loud to quiet.

Ingredient Two: Pitch, perceived on a spectrum from low to high.

Ingredient Three: Pitch Fluctuation, perceived as being fast or slow, great or small.

Ingredient Four: Register, perceived as either modal, falsetto or blended.

Ingredient Five: Harmonic Timbre, which can be Flute, Clarinet or Saxophone.

Ingredient Six: Violin, perceived on a spectrum from minimum to maximum.

Ingredient Seven: Free Air, perceived on a spectrum from minimum to maximum.

Ingredient Eight: Attack, perceived on a spectrum from lesser to greater.

Ingredient Nine: Disruption, perceived on a spectrum from mild to severe.

Ingredient Ten: Articulation, perceived as a sculpturing of the voice into vowels and consonants.

A Methodology for Training, Therapy and Analysis

These ten components of vocal expression form the core of the Voice Movement Therapy system which is both an analytic profile for interpreting voices, a psychotherapeutic means by which to investigate the way psychological material is communicated through specific vocal qualities, a training system for developing the expressiveness of voices and a physiotherapeutic means by which to release the voice from functional misuse.

The ten components of vocal expression offers a framework within which all voices can be analysed. However, the most significant use of this system is not simply to analyse what one hears, but to enable a single human voice to acquire the dexterity with which to manifest manifold combinations of vocal qualities. When this is achieved, the voice is able to serve both artistic procedures by bringing greater vocal flexibility to the process of singing and is also able to express a greater range of emotional and psychological experience. Voice Movement Therapy is therefore predicated upon a synthesis of analytic, artistic and therapeutic principles.

The set of ten vocal components offers a framework of analysis within which voice production can be analysed intuitively in the absence of objective measuring equipment. For with training it is possible for an attentive listener to sense the composite combination of the ten components which may be present in a voice at any given time. Those who train in Voice Movement Therapy can therefore learn to hear the voice as comprising a set of vocal tract dimensions and their consequent acoustic timbres known as Flute, Clarinet and Saxophone which can be articulated across a range of pitches, each of which can fluctuate to some degree. These sounds can all be vocalised with degrees of loudness, with a greater or lesser amount of attack and with a spectrum of more or less Free Air, creating a sound which may be to some degree disrupted and produced in a certain vocal register with a greater or lesser amount of Violin.

The various combinations of these components are obviously manifold, each giving specific vocal qualities expressive of particular artistic styles and with particular psychological connotations. Because these vocal components are rooted in the elementary physiological and mechanical operation of the voice, they can be applied with equal efficacy whether analysing vocal expression in a therapeutic setting or vocal styles in an artistic context.

Because the practitioner is approaching the voice subjectively, intuitively drawing upon his or her own responses in the absence of empirical measuring procedures, the Voice Movement Therapy system provides a non-judgemental framework in which to locate such responses. For it is always tempting to analyse the voice by labelling sounds according to emotional, figurative or attitudinal constructs which emanate from the practitioner's own associations. This gives rise to descriptive terms such as 'whiny', 'depressive', 'bubbly', 'child-like', 'aggressive' or 'weak'. In contradistinction to this approach is the provision of measuring devices and the clinical language of allopathic systems which describes the voice with terms based in physiological pathology, such as 'hyperkinetic' and 'whispered aphonia'. Whilst the former acknowledges the emotionality and imaginative capacity of the voice, it risks a dangerous disconnection from the mechanics of voice production and can potentially perpetuate a prejudicial reinforcement of vocal stereotyping. The latter, meanwhile, has the advantage of being grounded in an objective understanding of mechanical and physiological voice production and avoids preconceived interpretative conclusions but, on the other hand, relies on scientific procedures and equipment and locates the voice in a language of medicinal pathology which has little to do with the creative and psychological function of vocal expression. The system of voice profile and analysis which I have designed offers an opportunity to walk the middle way between these two approaches.

The analytic and interpretative use of the system requires the practitioner to translate associative subjective responses to the vocalist into a profile based on the vocal ingredients. With training, this is possible with some ease because it is these ingredients to which we attend unconsciously when interpreting voices. We may believe someone to be angry because their voice becomes disrupted, the speed of their pitch fluctuation increases, as the sound becomes loud and deep in pitch. We may believe someone is joyous and excited because their voice breaks out of Modal into Falsetto as it rises in Pitch and the quantity of Free Air increases as the vocal tract lengthens and dilates into Saxophone Configuration. We may think someone is frightened because their voice has a rapid pitch fluctuation and is very quiet with little attack. We may believe someone to be pessimistic and despondent because their voice is infused with Violin and Free Air within a very small pitch range and is produced with the narrow and shortened vocal tract of Flute Configuration. This system enables the practitioner to suspend supposition regarding the emotional experience or personality characteristics allegedly expressed and ascertain the vocal ingredients.

We also listen unconsciously to these ingredients when we hear different singers. Some vocalists utilise Free Air, others have very disrupted voices. Some types of song are well suited to the expanded Saxophone dimensions of the vocal tract, whilst others require the contained nature of the Flute Configuration. Furthermore, the singing styles and voice production techniques indigenous to a specific culture tend to favour certain combinations of ingredients. This component system of intuitive analysis therefore also aims to provide a framework within which various cultural and artistic styles of singing can be located.

The pedagogical use of the system requires the practitioner to teach clients how to attain sufficient malleability of the vocal instrument to be able to combine all vocal ingredients, thereby having at their disposal the broadest possible vocal palette for professional, artistic and personal use. In order to facilitate this in others it is absolutely essential for practitioners to possess such malleability themselves. A significant part of the accredited training programmes in Voice Movement Therapy is therefore focused upon training the student's own voice to manifest a broad range of vocal component combinations. Subsequent to the acquisition of this ability, trainees learn the strategies by which to facilitate maximum vocal expressiveness in others.

The process of teaching voice naturally involves investigating both the physical and the psychological reasons for the particular limitations to a client's voice. The application of this system therefore involves a certain therapeutic process on a somatic and psychological level which requires of the practitioner a compassionate, humanitarian and empathic response to the vocal process at all times.

In the following and final chapter, I will document some case studies which reveal the pedagogical and therapeutic use of this system to assist the client's healing process.

CHAPTER 6

Journeys Through Song
Case Studies in the Use of Voice Movement Therapy

Voice and Self-Identity

The set of ten vocal constituents which make up the core of the Voice Movement Therapy method provides a coherent model for working with clients through the medium of singing. Its primary therapeutic value rests in the fact that when clients produce a particular combination of vocal components for the first time, they listen to a part of their Self as though for the first time and experience a radical shift of self-image, identity and self-perception. New sounds create new identities, for the voice acts as an acoustic mirror which reflects back to the vocalist an image of the Self in sound.

The material of the voice is sensual and sensory. We hear it through the senses. Frequently we hear the voice as though through the sense of touch. We feel pinched, slapped, compressed, pierced, hammered, stroked, tickled, or shaken by a voice. We hear the voice as though through the sense of taste, listening to the despondent bitterness, the citrus tang of jealousy or the sugary sycophantic sweetness. We hear the colour of a voice, the deep blue of melancholia, the green of envy and the red of retaliation. We may also feel the temperature of a voice, which can be experienced as warm, cool, burning hot or ice cold. But it is not just the listener's senses which are affected by the voice. Often, the presence of a particular vocal quality also affects the way the vocalist perceives herself. Our own voice feeds back messages to us through our own ears. Our voice reaffirms who we are, how we are feeling and what we are seeking. The voice serves an important function in maintaining our sense of identity, for the sound of our voice reminds us of who we are, it reinforces our sense of Self. In the same way that our identity is continually reaffirmed by the visual reflection provided by a mirror, so too the sound of our voice enables us to hear reflected an audible expression of our own image.

Consequently, changing the voice has the potential to alter both the way others perceive us and the way we perceive ourselves.

As time passes we often become over-identified with a single image of ourselves. We become dominated by the image of our self as a particular character. We may become stuck in a child-like image, in a dominating and bombastic image, in a kindly and self-effacing image. And all of these self-images find expression through the quality of vocal tones.

Because the echo of the tone of our voice in our own ears is so important in reaffirming our own image, we become caught in a vicious circle. The bitterness or anxiety which we hear in our voice serves only to reinforce the image of ourselves as bitter or anxious. The childlikeness or aggressiveness which we hear in our voice reinforces the idea of our self as a child or an aggressor. If our psyche becomes so saturated with a single emotional tone, it may become difficult for us to communicate anything else and, without warning, the voice simply lets us down. We may wish to express a particular emotion or image, such as anger or authority; or we may need to instil confidence or calm. But, our voice has become so identified with a particular aspect of ourselves that it cannot move. It is as though the voice has become a rigid mask which we are unable to take off. A person with such a mask may feel mature but sound child-like, may feel enraged but sound intimidated, may feel saddened but sound unmoved; they seek help but their voice signals self-certainty; they seek warmth and affection, but their voice signals guarded detachment; they seek respect but their voice attracts belittlement. Often this can cause the person some distress, for what people hear on the outside bears no relation to what the person feels on the inside.

Expanding the range of the voice and allowing it to dance freely through all of its colours provides us with an opportunity to step outside the fixity of our familiar mask and reanimate the entire kaleidoscope of our personality. Psychologically, this enables us to visit and express those parts of the Self which have hitherto remained in the dark and undercover.

To do this it is necessary to peel back the layer of spoken words which keeps deep emotion under wraps. We must once again allow the voice to holler and roar, screech and lament. By transforming the voice in this way, we can effect changes in the sense of Self. We can provide an opportunity for every individual to hear themselves afresh. Then, when someone can hear themselves as something more than the familiar limited personality to which they have become accustomed, this new refreshed person can be voiced outwardly in the world for others to hear.

Working through the singing rather than the speaking voice brings a highly emotionalised dimension to this process. When a client discovers a new set of ingredients, often the sound brings with it a tirade of emotion, often connected to experiences from the distant past which have remained unexpressed for a long time.

Singing provides at once both a catalyst and container for such intense emotional experience. Singing allows for the discharge of emotions of greater magnitude and longevity than talking. Yet singing also provides an artistic framework which protects the client from becoming overwhelmed by the products of an unsculptured catharsis of their pain.

Voice and Emotion

Many people seek therapeutic help of one kind or another because they reach a realisation that they can no longer carry the burden of intense psychological pain. Each verbal and linguistic language has a different word for pain. Indeed, each language has a different word for sadness and happiness, for fear and panic, for love and hate, for joy and sorrow. Yet, the vocal sounds which express such universal emotions are recognisable in every culture and in every society regardless of the language spoken.

When someone needs to express pain or anguish with authenticity and intensity, verbal language is of little use; for psychological pain emanates from a level of the psyche which is preverbal, transverbal and archetypal. An authentic expression of trauma necessitates vocal but non-verbal expression which means a return to an infantile mode of expression. For the newly born infant, life after the 'birth trauma' is a series of 'little traumas': the trauma of sudden changes of temperature; the trauma of hunger; the trauma of abandonment when the mother leaves the room; the trauma of radical changes in acoustic environment as the ear adjusts to the impedance of air. And the psychological anguish which these traumas cause is expressed directly through vocal cries, wails and screams.

The preverbal infant does not translate or de-scribe his experience into a verbal culturally conditioned code; he gives direct expression to it through sound. However, once the child learns to speak, from that point on even the most intense emotional experiences will have to be named, worded and articulated in order to be communicated and accepted.

Yet for many people, the contents of the heart are simply beyond, beneath or above words. In addition to the burden of living with the trauma of unhealed pain, many people therefore face the further torment that their pain remains invisible because it cannot be spoken. For such people, providing an opportunity for vocal expression through sound offers an effective vehicle for healing.

One of the oldest and most well-established models of mind–body functioning is the cathartic paradigm. According to a cathartic view, the human organism is a hydraulic system capable of receiving and dispensing energy. Energy enters and leaves the psychic and somatic system in a variety of ways. Energy can enter the body through the ears, so that when someone shouts at us, verbally abuses us or whispers sweet words of love to us, the energy in our system is increased. The same amount of energy may then be dispensed from our system if we verbally retaliate, punch our verbal aggressor or return the loving compliment with a kiss. Energy can also enter the system through the eyes. If we are exposed to a terrifying sight or if we set our eyes upon something of incredible beauty, then our psychic energy is increased. And this energy can be released through our behavioural reactions, such as running away screaming or singing the praises of the beauty which we behold.

The cathartic model proposes that to maintain health, the system must be kept in a state of energetic balance. Moreover, to keep the system in a state of balance, the same amount of energy which enters the system must in turn be released. However, there are many factors which prevent this from occurring: fear, intimidation, shock and a host of social prohibitions often prevent people from responding equally to the energetic events which influence them. As a result, a build-up of psychic energy occurs, causing an increase in pressure within the system.

Many people experience psychological pain because they have been traumatised either by a single event or by an ongoing situation; and the consequent pain is often the result of an accumulation of emotional energy which has not been discharged. A cathartic therapy is one which provides someone with an opportunity to discharge this accumulated energy in a safe place, as though reliving the original trauma but where the person is enabled to react to it and to retaliate.

When someone is offered an opportunity for catharsis, it is as though the emotional floodgates come bursting open and a historic backlog of unexpressed pain comes flowing out, leaving the person with a sense of having been relieved, perhaps even purged.

In order for a genuine catharsis to be facilitated, there has to be an open channel through which psychic energy can be released – and the voice provides such a channel.

The human voice is basically one long continuous tube which begins at the lips, becomes the mouth, curls down to become the throat, continues downwards into the neck becoming the larynx and travels on down into the chest where it splits into two tubes, one passing into each lung. There is then the sense that the voice is capable of bringing things up from deep inside the body.

Vocal catharsis involves allowing a person to vocalise a gamut of sounds which are emotionally charged and which depressurise the energetic system by discharging emotions which have hitherto remained contained. Such a process may be referred to as 'anti-singing'; that is to say that the person is taught to vocalise in such a way as to produce not the voice of beauty appropriate to the aesthetics of the concert hall but a voice which gives authentic acoustic form to pain through the non-beautiful voice. During a vocal cathartic process within Voice Movement Therapy the client may sob, wail, scream, bemoan, holler and screech as previously unexpressed trauma is given shape through sound. This means that the practitioner plays the role of a singing teacher, facilitating the client in acquiring a palette of sounds from which to draw when vocalising extreme emotional material.

But, to be effective, a therapeutic process cannot end in a catharsis; and a process which uses voice as a primary channel of expression cannot end in the silence which follows the echo of vocalised pain. As the client discharges emotion through sound and movement it is paramount that the practitioner can seize the moment when sounds of anguish can become sounds of triumph, when sounds of intimidation can become sounds of victory, when sounds of horror can become sounds of joy and when sounds of grief can become sounds of hope.

From Catharsis to Creativity

One of the problems with a cathartic therapy is that the relief experienced can turn out to be short-lived and the psychic and somatic manifestation of trauma can quickly reconstellate as vigorously as before. This can lead to a cyclical dependency on some kind of cathartic release where the client is never really free from a repetitious return to an original hurt.

In my experience, in order for the cathartic relief to be long-lasting, the client must be enabled to take hold of the discharged emotion, transform it and, most importantly, make conscious expressive use of it. In this way, a certain artistic distance is created between the client as generator of emotional content and the client as a conscious sculptor of emotional form.

To understand the concept of 'artistic distance' and its therapeutic value it is useful to consider the art of the singer. In the course of an evening concert, a singer may sing a variety of emotionally charged songs from up-tempo, light-hearted love songs to sorrowful ballads of desperation. In one song the singer may be beaming with a smile and genuinely feel full of glee as she sings; in the very next song the singer may weep and be genuinely full of sadness. Yet there is distance between the experience of emotion and the sculpturing of that emotion to form a song. Indeed, the song itself acts as a formed container for emotion which, otherwise, may pour endlessly from the voice without end.

If the singer is also the writer of her own songs, there may be a time, during the original writing of the song, when the singer is overwhelmed with emotion, particularly if she is drawing the song from her own traumatic experience. In many ways, the writing of the song may provide for a certain catharsis. But the art of the singer does not stop at this catharsis. The healing occurs in the next phase where the song can be sung with enough recollected authenticity of the original trauma to ensure an emotive realism but with enough distance to ensure that the rendition of the song is artful. This is what I have called 'artistic distance'.

One of the most important things which this artistic distance provides is the ability to reap pleasure from pain. For the singer will experience the act of singing as highly pleasurable whilst at the same time experiencing something of the pain which the song may describe. Indeed, many singers will testify that the more painful the subject of the song the more pleasure is reaped from singing it. It is as though singing enables us to link arms with pain and remember its inevitable place in our life without finding our self immovably clasped by its grip.

The client of a therapeutic process which uses voice as a primary medium, such as Voice Movement Therapy, may be compared to the singer. At first, a flood of sound is poured out, giving acoustic shape to deep emotion, very often of an extremely painful kind. But in time, this outpouring is familiar enough to be heard as the rudiments of a song and can be formed. It can be given melodic structure, rhythm and words. At this point, the client is not only freed from a cycle of cathartic discharge but he is also, to a large extent, free of the interventions of the practitioner. The client can now move the body through space and guide the voice through the contours of the acoustic palette, creating an authentic song and dance from the fresh vitality which is uncovered by the release of pain – and the practitioner at this point is primarily a witness.

But it is this transition from the release of pain to the discovery of pleasure that presents the practitioner with the most difficult and sensitive task. In fact, in my opinion, facilitating the vocalisation of pain is relatively a straightforward procedure. But enabling that pain to be relinquished and reinvented in the form of a genuine healed Self requires great diligence, patience and sensitivity. For, if one attempts to heal pain too early, too quickly or too superficially, then the hurt Self feels patronised, belittled and poorly nursed and will, in an attempt to survive, persist all the more adamantly. On the other hand, if the hurt Self is encouraged to discharge itself continually without progression to an artistic mode of expression, the process of catharsis will serve only to feed the very pain that it seeks to heal.

In dealing with clients whose primary need is the expression and transformation of psychological pain, the Voice Movement Therapy practitioner is therefore in the combined role of psychotherapist, singing teacher and physical therapist. This means that the practitioner focuses simultaneously on a number of tasks. First, she must be able to offer a compassionate understanding of the client's expressions; second, she must be able to teach the client to release emotion through sound which balances authenticity of emotion with healthy use of the vocal instrument; third, she needs to be able to manipulate the client's body in order to assist the surmounting of somatised trauma; and fourth, she must be able to lead the client to a place of artistic distance from which the healed Self may experience a pleasure greater than the pain of the hurt Self. If the practitioner can combine these tasks, then a client suffering from the consequences of psychological pain can be offered a therapeutic process with genuine healing potential.

Singing then offers an opportunity to work psychotherapeutically with the two primary materials of the Self: emotion and identity. In this chapter, I will offer some case studies which throw some light on the way that the Voice Movement Therapy system enables clients to work transformatively on themselves through the medium of the sung voice.

Case Study: Richard

I Heard the Plane Come Down

Richard, whom I introduced earlier, was one of a few who had survived an aeroplane crash. Though he had remarkably and miraculously not sustained any serious physical injury, the event had severe consequences regarding his mental and emotional life.

His symptoms included insomnia, nightmares, periods of extreme depression, suicidal fantasies and panic attacks. Prior to the accident he had been married and held a job carrying considerable responsibility at a major financial institution. However, he had never returned to work and one year after the crash he was divorced.

Richard had received counselling twice a week for the first three months after the accident and once a week for a further two months. Since then he had not pursued any further therapy, but visited his general practitioner frequently for a variety of medications including analgesics and tranquillisers.

Prior to the accident, Richard had been a member of a choir where he often sang solo and which was his central social and recreational pursuit. Since the accident, however, he had not sung and said that he felt as though his voice had dropped out of him. Before the accident, Richard had been an outspoken person with a loud and resonant voice. Now, his speaking voice was almost a whisper and he felt nervous when called upon to speak up for himself. Richard had come into therapy because he wanted to refind his singing voice in order that he could rejoin a choir and 'begin to put his life back together'. Moreover, he was somewhat guarded about working directly on the experience of the accident because he said he had 'been through it over and over again in counselling'.

The only optical memory which Richard had of the plane crash was seeing the head of the person he was sitting adjacent to separate from his body. The rest was, he said 'complete darkness' until he was placed upon a stretcher by the medical team. What Richard did have was a complete spectrum of acoustic memories: engine noises, announcements of the pilot, the screams of the passengers and the sirens of the emergency team. Indeed, when Richard told the story, most of his sentences which described the three minutes leading up to the point of impact – at which he became buried by debris and contained by darkness – began with the words: 'I heard'.

For example, he said 'I heard the pilot announce his apologies for the difficult take-off'; he said 'I heard the crashing of the glasses in the steward area'; he said 'I heard the sirens of the emergency team and I knew I was alive'; and he said 'I heard someone say: "It's all right, we are going to get you out."'

I could not help being struck by the rhythm and tonality of the repetitious use of the motif 'I heard' which began each of his sentences. I therefore asked Richard to write them down in a long list and read them out aloud. He read:

I heard the engine rumble

I heard the plane jolt

I heard the captain say there was a problem

I heard the passengers cry

I heard the woman behind me praying

I heard the scraping of metal on tarmac

I heard the tyres skidding

I heard sirens whistling

I heard someone ask if I could hear them

I heard the plane come down

Richard then found a melody for these lyrics by amplifying the natural prosody of his speech.

At first, the voice with which he sang the song was very quiet, in a middle Pitch range with a vibrato – or fast pitch fluctuation – in modal register. After the first rendition, I asked Richard to recall the sound of metal on tarmac and to allow this image to influence the timbre of the voice. I suggested that he infuse the voice with Violin, take away the pitch fluctuation and increase the loudness. When he did this, the entire ambience of the song changed and Richard became highly mobilised as the song became like a combination of Marching Song, Folk Ballad and Protest Song. The Violin component gave the song an edge and Richard said that the Violin quality made him feel strong and hard, like a soldier who had survived a battle. The wounds were still there but there was an incredible sense of relief.

Keeping the Violin quality, I began leading Richard up the pitch scale on single notes until his voice broke into falsetto register. I asked Richard to think of the whistling sirens which he had heard when the medical team had attended the scene of the accident. His voice ascended until he was high in the altitude of his pitch range and he now sang the song in a piercing whistle-like voice. This voice was loud, high in pitch, in falsetto register and with a moderate amount of Free Air. As he sang in this voice, tears ran down his cheeks, yet he stood absolutely motionless.

Richard said that this voice encapsulated the total fear and helplessness which he had experienced during the accident: the word he used was 'mesmerised'. The Free Air had brought a softness and vulnerability to the voice which had made him cry. It was the first time he had actually cried since the accident. Richard said that he had been 'crying inside' since the accident but had not been able to let his tears out.

We now worked on the song combining both the high voice which had a lot of Free Air and which made him feel helpless and the lower voice with had a lot of Violin which made him feel strong and relieved. As he sang the song, he blended the two voices together, moving from phrases of exquisite vulnerability to phrases of powerful declamation. He sang the song many times and used the various components of his voice to express fear and rage, sorrow and triumph.

When this work was over, Richard felt that he had at last managed to 'bring into the open' feelings and images which, since the accident, had remained 'inside'. The singing of the event was very different to the talking about the event which he had done in earlier therapy. And, most importantly, he had been able to cry, and with his tears came the expression of emotions which had been buried for a long time.

Case Study: John

Of Mice and Men

Unfortunately there are many whose tears have dried up in the heat of life's scorching blaze and who, knowingly or not, suffer the impoverishment which comes with the absence of weeping. Yet everyone can reclaim their ability to cry and the impulse may be provoked by something seemingly trivial. For when we are children, our tears are not provoked by tragedies of enormity but by the little things which are so important to us when we are little ourselves.

A man called John whom I once worked with provides a touching example of the magnitude of such small remembered things. John was a clear, confident and eloquent speaker and felt at ease introducing himself to the Voice Movement Therapy group. He could raise his voice in Loudness with no trouble; he could assert both his strength and his opinions and could readily mobilise himself to anger, which he expressed through the booming resonant tones of his voice. However, John did not cry. In fact, John confessed that he never felt sadness, sorrow or any sensation that might move him to tears; and this had started to bother him. His healing journey was to reclaim his weeping.

On the first day of the group process John had written a song about a pet rabbit which he had when he was a child. On the second day, I worked with John individually and asked him to sing a single note gently into the palm of his hand and to imagine that he had a wounded rabbit in his palm. His voice was in modal register with quite a lot of Violin, in Clarinet timbre but with no Free Air. As John sang, I asked him to mime stroking the rabbit with his other hand. To see this six-foot tall man with shoulders broad enough to bear a nation uttering such sweet and gentle tones was a truly stirring sight.

As John sang I noticed tiny rhythmical spasms in his abdomen and so I placed my hand gently on his belly. As I did this he let out a long sigh as though something had changed gear. His voice now undulated with a gentle pitch fluctuation and became full of Free Air, as though a gate had opened allowing his breath to come pouring through. I asked John to raise the pitch of the note and to decrease the loudness, as though he did not want to frighten the tiny creature in his hand. I suggested that he was the Rabbit Healer, a lone outcast that lived in the forest without human contact but who could communicate with the animals. He looked at me with inquisitive resonance as though in an uncanny way I had touched on something close to his heart. John's voice now began to break between modal and falsetto register; his shoulders hunched and he began walking around the studio, as though alone in the forest. John began singing the words to his song in this new voice that was quiet, high in pitch with a gentle fluctuation, full of Free Air and which sobbed back and forth between the two registers.

> Gentle one you have been hurt and no one really knows
> At the bottom of the garden we talk in rabbit speak
> and our friendship grows
> My world is hidden between these trees
> I don't like boys or girls
> But to be alone with my tiny friends
> Is all I really need

John said that he felt embarrassed by his song and the triviality of the memory; yet he was clearly choked and I supported him in continuing to sing. Then, in the middle of the song as his voice broke out of modal into falsetto, John began to cry. The more he cried, the more emotive and

provocative his voice became and a number of people in the witnessing group were now also moved to tears.

John later said that whilst singing into the palm of his hand he had remembered how, as an only child who was awkward and often ridiculed at school, he had found solace in animals. In particular, he remembered playing for hours at the bottom of the garden where he would talk to his rabbits in a pretend make-believe language. Somehow this simple memory, provoked by finding the space to place his body and voice back in that garden, had unlocked tender emotions which he had not allowed himself to express since he was a child: feelings of loneliness, sorrow, and despair.

Case Study: Teri

Daddy's Little Princess

Teri came into therapy because she felt her voice was too high in pitch, too 'breathy' and too 'child-like'. She worked as a clerk at a law firm and a number of her colleagues had told her that her voice sounded childish. She had applied for the promotion due to her three times; and three times she had failed. Had she been awarded the post she sought, for which she was amply experienced and qualified, it would have involved a considerable amount of telephone contact with clients. She felt that the sound of her voice was the main reason that she had missed promotion.

Teri had chosen to work through Voice Movement Therapy in the hope that it might enable her to lower the pitch of her voice and to sound 'more mature'. At the same time she was a little worried because her boyfriend liked her voice and she was concerned that she might lose his affections if her voice changed too much.

As Teri explained her story I noticed that her speaking voice did create the impression of naïveté and susceptibility; and her entire demeanour was very pubescent. When Teri began to sing a long continuous note I noticed that she placed her hands together in front of her and protruded her hips to one side. Her voice was in Flute timbre, high in pitch, in falsetto register with lots of Free Air and a moderate amount of Violin. As I listened and watched she reminded me of Marilyn Monroe, whom she said she had always admired.

Teri's parents had separated when she was eight years old and she had lived permanently with her father, visiting her mother for one day twice a month. Her mother had been an alcoholic as well as suffering from intermittent mental illness. Teri had one brother, four years her senior, who went away to college when he was 16. Teri had therefore lived alone with her father from the age of 12 until she left home at 18. Teri loved her father; she almost idolised him. He had protected her, cherished her, doted on her every smile, succumbed to her every wish and provided for her every need – so long as she remained his little girl. When she reached adolescence and began to want the freedom to explore the world beyond the exclusivity of the paternal dotage, her father had not been so good at letting her go as he had been at keeping her near.

In preparation for the next session I asked Teri to find two songs which reflected some of the aspects of her therapeutic journey. The next session she returned with 'My Heart Belongs to Daddy' – immortalised by Marilyn Monroe – which she had practised to the gleeful and supporting admiration of her boyfriend; and 'Come on Baby, Light my Fire', which her boyfriend had said was 'too low and too aggressive' for her. When she sang 'My Heart Belongs to Daddy' her natural light, frivolous, pubescent voice effervesced as she imbued the song with the tantalising charismatic enticement of a coquette. When it came to singing 'Come on Baby, Light my Fire' she had more difficulty at first because she could not lower the pitch of the voice and create the rich, deep resonant tonal colour that she wanted. So I asked her to go in the opposite direction and to sing it extremely high in an exaggerated child-like voice, as though the young girl inside her was protesting in a tantrum of indignation and demand. I asked her to increase the amount of Violin and the amount of Free Air and, as Teri sang the song, I kept enabling her to go a little higher. With each ascending note, Teri's persona became more unruly as she located her indomitable spirit. I suggested to her that we seemed to be uncovering the defiant and recalcitrant juvenile behind the pliable fledgling damsel. As she sang higher and higher so she became rambunctious and intemperate, her arms splayed like the wings of an eagle, her lips curled back to expose the gnashing of her teeth and each word of the song pierced the room of my consulting room like a series of gold darts.

When we paused, Teri was both enlivened and disturbed. She said that she had never in all her life expressed such power, such wildness and such vitality. But she said that she felt very scared because finding this part of herself reminded Teri of her mother. Teri had not only been over-protected, mollycoddled and girlified by a father who wanted his daughter to remain his princess and replace the sweet wife he had lost to wild abandon. She had also been discouraged from expressing any kind of voracious or intemperate

feelings because it reminded her father too much of Teri's mother. In fact, Teri recalled a number of times when her father had told her that if she continued to 'behave that way' she would 'end up' like her mother. In many ways, Teri kept herself from growing up and finding the voice of a woman because her first and most potent experience of a woman was her mother who had been presented as crazy, out of control and incapable. Teri did not want to become her mother, so she played into the hands of her father and remained a little girl and from here she went into the lap of her boyfriend who was 12 years older than her and who encouraged the same child-like parts of her.

As Teri and I began to fit the pieces together she burst into tears of fury and began yelling at her mother: 'Where were you? Where were you?' Her breathing became deeper and her face was awash with tears as I heard her voice drop by at least an octave. This new voice was in Saxophone timbre, low in pitch in modal register with no Free Air and very little Violin. This was the voice she had been looking for. Teri's voice tube had probably never expanded so much in all her life. The Saxophone timbre was so unfamiliar to Teri that, at one point, she stopped and said 'Is that really me?'.

I asked Teri to write some spontaneous lyrics for a song which expressed the feelings behind her tears. She wrote:

> In your mad attic far away from me
> I cannot reach you though you're always in my dreams
> With your eyes glazed and your tongue wild
> My father keeps you hidden in case you infect me
> I want to grow up not to be like you
> But I don't know who you are and miss you every day
> Mother won't you come and rescue me
> Better to be crazy in your arms than sanely on my own
> I'm lonely and afraid though father loves me so
> Where were you, where are you, it's not fair you had to go

As she read the song over and over, she turned the prosody of her speech into a melody. She now sang the song in a deep exuberant and ebullient tone which washed through the consulting room like a river of molten chocolate. Her hands rested upon her belly as the tonal colour of her voice became increasingly sumptuous and rounded. This was a voice which crackled with the sediment of a mature red wine; this was a voice with the power to intoxicate and ignite; this was a voice aflame with fire.

Teri had discovered that she could release the voice of her matured invincible spirit without going mad; she had realised that though her father loved her he had also belittled her; and she declared that her vocal telephone manner would not be quite the same again. During the time I worked with Teri two things occurred. She was promoted to the post she had wanted; and she parted from her boyfriend. The one event brought her great joy; the other great sorrow. Yet, Teri felt convinced that she could not grow within the confines of her boyfriend's needs any more than she had been able to transcend her girlhood within the parameters of her father's expectations. So she moved on and cleared the road ahead with a voice of depth and courage.

Our voice is affected by the way it is heard; and sometimes we silence a whole range and spectrum of timbral colours because those whom we love find them difficult to hear. It is sad but true that sometimes we have to take our leave of those we love if we are to be free to voice who we really are. For if others can only love a few notes in the melody of our Self, then they cannot love us truthfully. We cannot be servants to song and give refrain only to the tunes which others require. For we need to sing the song of our own Self. But if we can have the courage to change our tune and sing our own serenade, allowing all our voices to emerge, then we can open our heart to the loving ears of those who want to hear us. A true voice attracts true love. This path is never easy and never without sadness and loss. But once the sonorous vibrations of change have been sounded, we cannot close our ears to them though life would seem easier if we could.

Case Study: Brigitte

The Good Woman

I once worked with a woman called Brigitte whose therapeutic journey involved the doleful and lamentable acknowledgement of her losses as well as the delightful and enchanted rediscovery of the spirit from which she had been separated. Hers was a journey which, like the journeys of many, touched the paradoxical core of tears which are shed in joy and sorrow simultaneously.

Brigitte was a good woman; she had been a good wife to her husband, a good mother to her two children and a good friend to all those in her circle. She had been hostess, envoy and confederate in attendance as she followed her husband around the globe in service of his profession. At diplomatic parties she had been beguiling and graceful, exalting her husband's name

and extolling the importance of his missions. She had stood at the side of rugby pitches and football grounds cheering her sons as they touched down and kicked off. She had listened to all of their stories, colluded in all of their antics and risen out of bed in the early hours of many mornings to fetch them back from the alcoholic parties of adolescent debauchery, placing toast and orange juice at their table before they fell asleep between the cotton sheets which she ironed with obedient regularity.

Now Brigitte's husband had retired and her boys had left the nest. Brigitte was lost, a little dazed and without the sense of purpose or function which had guided her for so long. She was in bereavement though nobody had died.

Brigitte began to make a sound. Her chest raised as she inhaled, her eyes sparkled and she intoned a long note which was fragile, light and quivered with a shaky tentativeness. Her voice was full of Free Air and pitch fluctuation and as she vocalised I placed my hand upon her chest and exerted a little pressure. This caused Brigitte's voice to increase substantially in loudness and as she sang I felt the imploring for reassurance in her eyes. 'It's OK,' I said, 'Just let it flow from your heart'. It was then that Brigitte emitted a tirade of sobbing. She blubbered and howled as her chest rose and fell like an elevator passing up and down through the tower of Babylon. Her face became showered with the waters of her tears. A backlog of feeling that had been stored up behind her eyes poured down like rain.

As she cried I noticed that her voice traced a five-note melody which she repeated each time she expired. Holding her close to me with my arm around her shoulders and my other hand still placed firmly upon her chest I sang the melody with her encouraging her to expand upon it. Within a few minutes she was singing and crying at the same time, her cheeks red, her eyes wet, her voice resounding like a bassoon. Her voice passed fluidly from low notes to high. In falsetto register her voice gleamed and shone like a golden fleece. In modal register her voice folded and churned like hot maple syrup. Then she stopped and began to laugh. I laughed with her. 'I don't know why I am crying,' Brigitte whispered as she chuckled, 'I am not really sad about anything'. I looked into her eyes and smiled and asked her if she could think of a song that we could work with. She mentioned 'Crying' which she had heard sung by Roy Orbison.

Brigitte stood tall, her eyes still damp and her cheeks still flushed and sang this song with poise and remorse, with zeal and yearning.

I was all right for a while
I could smile for a while
But when I saw you last night
You held my hand so tight
When you stopped to say hello
You wished me well
You couldn't tell
That I'd been crying over you

The group watched and listened and in the moments after the song came to its end there was a viscous silence which preceded the appreciative applause.

Later that day, Brigitte spoke of how she felt in some way bereaved. She had laid down so much of herself in order to serve her husband and sons and in the process had lost her voice in a family of male voices. Now her husband and sons no longer pulled upon her service, she also felt bereaved of her role as mother and wife. Her identity had melted and there seemed nothing to take its place. Her crying had been both an expression of her grief and at the same time a reclaiming of her own voice of feminine pathos. It was herself that she was crying over. She had always wanted to hear herself sing but never thought she could, never thought she would.

Case Study: Anne

I Do Like to Be Beside the Seaside

Anne's first glance at the world was through the confining walls of a plastic incubator. But that was not all. During the period when most children are beginning to talk, Anne was very sick and spent the majority of her second and third year in and out of a hospital crib.

Apparently, her mother was an anxious woman who, after Anne's birth, lived with the knowledge that her baby might die. Throughout Anne's life, her mother had been over-protective, as though she never quite recovered from the possibility of losing her daughter. As a result, Anne had entered adult life with little worldly wisdom. She was extremely shy, lacking in self-confidence and described herself as very quiet.

Anne worked as a secretary in a shipping office. She was reasonably happy but felt that people saw her as insignificant. Anne's speaking voice was quiet, high in Pitch and full of Free Air and she had a habitual gesture of brushing the fringe of her hair out of her eyes and across her forehead.

Anne found entering conversations very difficult. She said that when a group of people were talking together, she felt as though she could wait forever for a door to open and let her in. Once she found her way through the door, however, she was able to talk freely, so long as the nature of the conversation was not competitive or argumentative. I asked Anne what she would change about herself if she could. She replied instantly that she would like to find a man whom she could love and who would love her in return; and she said that in order to do this she felt she needed to be more able to express her strength and aggression.

When I first asked Anne to make a long open sound, she sang a note which was, to my ears, melancholic, romantic and sombre. Her voice was high in pitch with lots of Free Air, in falsetto register and Clarinet timbre with just a smattering of Violin. I asked her to journey around her voice making playful child-like sounds. She sang beautiful light notes on 'do bee doo tum be go la woo'. She giggled and remarked on how simple and yet how enjoyable it felt to do this. As I listened to Anne sing, it aroused in me the image of Audrey Hepburn or Grace Kelly standing on a bridge in the arms of a chivalrous gentleman. I asked Anne to allow the notes to wander up and down and suggested that she sing with an air of romance. As her voice began weaving gently and graciously a little higher and a little lower, Anne began to weep.

Anne had never had a relationship with a man, although she was 26 years old. She wanted love, the love of a man. She desired to contact her strength and aggression because she believed this would prevent her from being ignored and enable her to seek a relationship confidently. But neither strength nor aggression was the goal. Love was.

As I knew that Anne loved to listen to music, I asked her to find some love songs before the next session and to learn the one which moved her the most. She arrived a week later with a piece of paper upon which were inscribed the words of 'The Way We Were'. As she sang this song I envisioned a young couple waltzing along a pier or a promenade accompanied by the lapping waves and a distant accordion. When I told her this, she smiled and recalled a time when her father had taken her to the seaside without her mother or her brother. In the evening, before returning home, her father had sat with her on the pier and he had taught her a song about a lonesome sailor. Anne had inherited her musical inclination from her father who had loved to sing and played accordion.

I now asked Anne to sing 'The Way We Were' a second time, imagining that she was once again on the pier singing to her father. She did this exquisitely; and as she sang, I noticed that the hand which usually brushed her fringe across her forehead was now stroking her upper chest, in the region of the heart. This choreographic sweeping movement which had drawn my attention from the beginning seemed to take on more depth now that her hand was upon her heart rather than her brow. But, before Anne reached the end of the song she stopped, began to cry and sob violently and then, in an instant, her sorrow turned to rage and she began yelling 'It isn't fair', over and over again.

Her mother had not only protected Anne from the outside world, but also from her father whom her mother had perceived as too coarse, crude and altogether a bad influence. Her parents divorced when Anne was 13 and her mother made it extremely difficult for her daughter to visit her father, whom Anne missed terribly. When Anne was 19, her father died suddenly in a boating accident.

Anne had not felt threatened by her father at all. In fact she remembered him as affectionate, warm and understanding. With regard to her mother, meanwhile, Anne could not remember ever being cuddled or kissed, held or sang to by her. She had gone from the womb to a plastic incubator and from the incubator to the cool and mechanical arms of her anxious mother.

I sat quietly but with my heart in full attendance while Anne yelled and screamed and raged. She seemed to be releasing so much previously unexpressed emotion. She felt so incensed at her mother for extinguishing the relationship Anne had with her father – a rage intensified by the fact that the man was now dead and it was all too late. At the same time her heart was drenched in grief for the father she almost had.

The sounds which Anne made were highly intense; her face was red, her eyes gleamed with the glare of a panther, her breathing was deep as a barrel and the walls shook with the volume of her voice. I wondered if anyone had been there for Anne in a way which permitted her to release such sound before.

When Anne eventually settled and we began talking, I pointed out that her voice had, during her rage, taken on a robust and retaliatory quality and I helped Anne rediscover this sound when we worked together the following week. This new voice was extremely loud, low in pitch, in Saxophone timbre and modal register and thundered with an extremely fast pitch fluctuation. Leading Anne down the scale, she found an altogether different sound to the

graceful voice of the young woman in love. This sound was ravenous, dark and enfolding. It was also low down in the range of a classical baritone as it flowed out of her like a deep dark river. I also noticed that Anne had replaced the stroking of her heart with a new dance. Both hands were now rubbing her belly in a circular motion as though this new sound somehow emerged from there.

The next time we worked Anne practised moving back and forth between the two sounds which she had discovered: the light romantic sound of love and the weighted, deep sound of rage. She slipped easily between the two and as she did this, I asked her to develop her hand-dance by touching her chest and then her belly. What had at first been a nervous repetitive gesture of brushing her fringe out of her eyes now took on balletic eloquence and proportion. As she sang in the light voice, she ran her palm over her chest and extended her arm outwards as though taking her heart upon her sleeve and offering love to her suitor. When she sang in the weighted voice, she caressed her belly as though damned up behind the walls of her abdomen was a powerful flood of determination.

The two distinct voices were highly significant for Anne. The light, high voice expressed a number of things. It was the voice of the little girl who had been denied the man she first loved, her father, who was both sailor and singer. But this was also the voice of a romantic young woman who had so much love to give and who was searching for a man to love her and not leave her as her father had done. Meanwhile, her low baritone voice encapsulated the rage against her mother whom she felt had suffocated her. It also, however, expressed the deep strength she had, a strength which she felt in her belly. This was not the strength of anger or aggression, it was not the voice of attack or revenge. This was a voice which expressed the strength inherent in the virtues of patience, perseverance and faithfulness.

When I saw Anne for our next session she told me that our work together had prompted her to visit her mother. She had felt that she somehow wanted to get beneath the rage and disappointment and find some warmth in the relationship.

To Anne's amazement, her mother disclosed that a year before Anne's birth she had lost her first baby to a hereditary illness at only eight months old. From that point on, there had been no affection between Anne's mother and father. Anne's father had begun drinking and had, in her mother's words, 'closed down and shut off'. From this conversation, Anne learned what her mother had endured and how her mother had lived with the fear of losing her second child whilst trying to sustain a marriage after the lights had gone out.

During the session, we worked on her voice, aiming to bring together the light romantic sound and heavy dark sound into a single quality. At the end, Anne said that she felt she had discovered the real sadness: that her mother and father could not have both taken her to the seaside as a family, that her father never again sang to his wife after the death of his first-born, that she only ever saw her mother's cool disposition without knowing how it had come to be.

Some weeks later, when we finished our work together, Anne said that she had noticed herself both giving and receiving more warmth and affection in her workplace. She found this strange as she had originally imagined that she needed to express herself more aggressively. Yet she was now actually extending her heart to her colleagues in a way that was both vulnerable yet strong. In return, her professional associates were smiling at her, asking if she was well, looking at her straight in the eye. Anne said she felt as though she was thawing out after a big chill.

I heard from Anne six months after her last session. She had fallen in love. I never did hear what happened, but whatever the outcome I like to imagine that Anne and her man made it to the seaside and found time to stand upon the pier and sing to the ocean.

Client's Account: Janice

Fear of Opening

Janice, whom I introduced in the first volume of this series (Newham 1999), was a professional musician. Her primary instrument is the French horn. At the height of her career when she was enjoying success as a much sought-after player, Janice was consecutively raped by three men one night on her way home after a concert. Two of the three men took turns to hold her to the ground whilst the other raped her.

Despite the severe physical pain and the extreme emotional shock, Janice could barely make a sound throughout her ordeal. She tried to scream but could only produce a muffled shout. Whenever her voice did get anywhere near being loud enough to be heard, her oppressors covered her mouth with their hands. As a result of her ordeal, Janice was unable to play with the orchestra for ten months, during which time she received counselling twice a week.

Since the ordeal she had suffered three main physical symptoms: a feeling that she had an iron bar running vertically down the centre of her torso, a feeling of constriction around the throat and constant breathlessness. In addition, her voice felt paralysed. She came into therapy to try and regain some vocal strength and overcome the breathlessness but she also hoped for some further emotional healing in relation to the consequence of her having been raped.

When Janice vocalised it was in Flute with a great deal of Free Air. The sound also had a gentle vibrato which created the quality associated with someone who is nervous, perhaps even afraid. Janice said that when she vocalised, especially on a long continuous note, she felt the 'iron bar' tingling all the way down her chest.

As Janice vocalised over a period of about 15 minutes, I massaged the area vertically descending from the base of her neck to the pit of her stomach as well as the musculature each side of her spine. As I massaged and Janice vocalised, we both moved in a dance which took its impulses from Janice's emotional journey.

During the massage, Janice went from fear, to rage, to triumph. At times she sobbed and shook, at times she yelled in despair and at other times she called out: 'Get away, get away'. As she called out these words: 'Get away', she held on to my arm with a vice-like grip, pulling me towards her.

When working with someone who has suffered the kind of trauma which Janice went through, the practitioner plays two roles in the fantasy of the client. First, in the case of Janice, being a man, I was in many ways representative of her assailants and during the session, Janice needed to identify me as the enemy in order to express her rage and anger vocally in a fashion that felt real. At the same time, I also represented the helper, the man that would save her from her assailants; she therefore needed to know that I would be there for her as she went through her intense experience.

As Janice called out: 'Get away, get away' and held on to my arm, I whispered to her: 'It's all right, I am right here'. At this point, she put her other hand on her chest and said that it was all tingling and going soft.

I asked her to lean over from the waist and imagine that the voice was pouring out of her like a liquid and she began vocalising in a series of long sounds like the siren on a ship. I asked her to imagine that she was singing down into a well and that her voice echoed in the open abyss. As she did this, I massaged her abdomen and in time, her voice opened into Saxophone. She was very hot and clammy and her breathing rate was very quick with the primary area of visible motility in the upper chest. I continued to massage her abdomen and encouraged her to breathe with abdominal expansion. This slowed down the breathing rate and increased the amount of inspired air.

Janice now came up to standing. Her face was red, her pupils were dilated and her hands and arms started thrashing about. As her arms gyrated, her voice whizzed round and round in siren-like sweeps. I placed my arms under hers and followed them about and it turned into a kind of martial arts dance. Janice began to make 'karate-like' movements with her arms and her voice took on an aggressive quality, punctuated with rhythmic bursts.

I now stood back and moved to her front where we could make eye contact. She said: 'I want to go up – can I?'. I said: 'Of course' and she started ascending the pitch range in Saxophone going all the way up to a piercing whistle which she sustained for about a minute before breathing and repeating it again. The piercing whistle-like scream went on and on as though it would never stop.

As she vocalised, I asked her to imagine that she was a great white bird, flying above the cool pacific sea, swooping and gliding, like a mythical creature from Wagner, and asked her to improvise a melody in this ultra-high range. She began to sing in a voice so clear and so high it would have made the audience at Covent Garden fall from their seats.

Her arm movements became wing movements and her voice whistled on.

Then I asked her to continue singing imagining that she was a bird of prey, swooping in her search for food. I wanted her to stop and settle on the ground, but she would not.

Eventually, Janice came to stillness and eventually rolled over onto the floor. She later told me that she was terrified that if she got onto her back on the floor her voice would go again and she would not be able to move. She was afraid of finding herself back in the paralysed silence of the rape again.

As Janice rolled over onto her back, her legs went up in the air, her arms gyrated and tore the air to shreds and her voice reached its crescendo. Then she leapt up onto her feet, sung out and fell back down to the floor again, rolling over on to her back. She went round and round this cycle, proving to herself that she could vocalise fully and move freely from the position she had been raped in to a triumphant standing position.

When she stopped, I asked Janice to take some time to sit and write a stream of words which expressed her experience and told her that we would use the words as the lyrics to a song.

She returned with:

> The iron in my chest
> The rage in my heart
> The blood in my cunt
> The poison in their eyes
> The sorrow in my soul
> The danger in my trust
> The ending of this tale
> Has now become a must
> Listen to my voice
> And let me live again

We now returned to vocalising in the high whistle in Saxophone timbre which she had discovered, but this time she sang the words – like a diva. Over the next few weeks, Janice wrote a number of songs and sang them, both in her sessions with me and on her own. Her breathlessness decreased and her voice returned; and she soon returned to playing in the orchestra.

When Janice's work with me came to an end she said that though the intensity of her catharsis in the sessions had been a core part of her healing, it was the channelling of the discharged emotions into her own songs which gave her the self-empowerment to move on. When we write and sing our own songs, the material of our pain takes artistic shape and becomes something more than the residue of our suffering; it becomes sacred, communicative and elevated.

Client's Song: Vicky

Ungluing the Voice

Finally, I will return to Vicky, whom I introduced earlier.

To recap, Vicky was repeatedly abused by her father who made her engage in oral sex. Her memories were very vivid, particularly the feeling of 'a numb helplessness' in her body as her father knelt on her arms to keep her down. Vicky came to work on herself through Voice Movement Therapy because, although psychotherapy had enabled her to deal with and overcome many of the issues and heal some of the damage, some problems remained. The main problem was a feeling of tightness in her throat and what she described as 'an incredibly inhibited voice'. Whenever she came to project her voice or speak up about something important, she would feel a 'stickiness' in her throat, as though her voice was 'covered with something' that made it 'dull and unable to flow fluidly'.

Early in her therapeutic process, Vicky had written and musicalised the following journey song:

> Sperm and cream it makes me scream
> Daddy made me suck his big Jimmy Dean
> My arms went dead and the voice in my head
> Told me to endure this sight obscene
> I was only little with no real choice
> Oh please God let me take the glue from my voice
> I have tried to fight and punch and kick
> To expel from my mouth his big salty prick
> But the more I try the more I cry
> And I choke and spew and people wonder why
> For Dad is dead and no one gets
> Why my voice is stuck and why I seem upset
> But if I feel quite safe and no one hurts me so
> I can relax my body and I start to let go
> And when I do my voice unglues
> And I start to hear myself afresh and anew

When Vicky sang the song, it was in Flute timbre, in falsetto register with a moderate amount of Free Air quite high in pitch. She now felt that she wanted to sing the song with a different quality of voice. She said that her voice sounded restricted and weak and that she felt like she wanted to get angry but did not know how.

I asked Vicky to increase radically the amount of Violin and to sing with a lot more loudness.

Her voice now sounded cutting and conjured in me the image of a razor blade. I asked her to ascend the Pitch scale, increasing the nasality of the voice imagining the sound was cutting through something. As she vocalised, the sound became machine-like and Vicky began marching on the spot. I asked her to swing her arms and imagine that she held a blade of some kind with which she was hacking back undergrowth. Her voice was now high in pitch and in falsetto register with a very fast pitch fluctuation and had opened into Saxophone timbre.

I then asked Vicky to continue vocalising, but this time without Violin. She attempted this but then complained that without this ingredient, she felt

weak and defenceless, whereas the presence of the Violin ingredient made her sound and feel empowered.

So, we now returned to her Journey Song and she sang it with various combinations of ingredients, but always with a lot of Violin. It sounded incredibly self-possessed and Vicky said that *this* was the voice of rage and retaliation which she had been looking for. In particular, the opening of the voice tube to Saxophone and the infusing of the voice with Violin created a vocal identity which she found very strengthening. In fact, she said that it sounded like a whole other person – a person that she said she wanted to get to know.

A Final Note

One of the main skills in Voice Movement Therapy is knowing which combination of vocal ingredients will enable a client to liberate a freedom of psychological expression. The ingredients which make up the Voice Movement Therapy system are not just acoustic entities which provide a convenient model of vocal analysis. The ingredients also act as emissaries for psychological and emotional material. Of course, we must beware of simplistic diagnostic paradigms where we fall into the trap of proposing that a particular vocal ingredient or combination thereof consistently expresses a specific psychic component. For the components of voice are utilised in unique ways by each person. However, one thing seems to be certain: the use of the vocal components provides the practitioner with a means of enabling the client to discover a malleability of vocal expression and provides the client with a language of self-revelation within which certain emotional experiences can be contained and expressed by specific sounds.

The aforementioned case studies provide an insight into the relationship between the spectrum of vocal sounds and the spectrum of human experience. It is for time to tell the diversity of client populations for whom such a method proves fruitful.

During the course of exploring different combinations of ingredients, many people, like Vicky, momentarily experience a shift of identity, as though encountering another character. In addition to the use of song, as described in this volume, Voice Movement Therapy also makes provision for the use of theatre by giving the client an opportunity to create dramatic characters which emanate from vocal identities. It is this specific use of theatre, rooted in an extensive use of the voice, which I will explore in the next volume of this series *Using Voice and Theatre: The Practical Application of Voice Movement Therapy.*

The Voice Movement Therapy System of Vocal Analysis

The System of Vocal Analysis

The following is a succinct recap of the ten ingredients which constitute the Voice Movement Therapy system of vocal analysis. Please note that the ingredients are presented in this Appendix in a different order to the order in which they are explained in Chapter Five. The use of the ingredients does not necessitate that they be fixed to a particular sequence and the numbers given to each ingredient are arbitrary.

Component One: Pitch

> Each vocal sound is perceived to have a certain pitch, note or fundamental tone, determined by the frequency of vocal cord vibration. This is perceived within the metaphor of high to low, though in fact it does not relate to spatial dimensions but to speed of vibration in time.

The initial sound which is shaped and coloured to produce a unique human voice is made by the vibration of the vocal cords. These two folds of tissue, also known as the vocal folds, lie stretched out in the larynx. At the front they are attached to the Adam's apple or thyroid cartilage and at the back they are connected to two movable cartilages called the arytenoids.

These two pieces of tissue are further attached to the trachea and the surrounding inner walls of the larynx by a complex set of muscles known collectively as the intrinsic laryngeal musculature. During normal breathing the vocal folds lie at rest, one each side of the larynx, like an open pair of curtains allowing air to pass freely through a window. The hole between the vocal folds through which air passes is called the glottis. However, adjustments in the distribution of tension in the laryngeal musculature can cause the vocal folds to close, preventing air from entering or leaving the trachea, like a thick pair of curtains drawn tightly shut across a window.

The sound of the human voice is generated by the rapid and successive opening and closure of the vocal cords many times per second and it is to this process that people refer when they speak of the vibration of the vocal cords. This rapid vibration of the vocal cords causes the expelled air from the lungs to be released through the glottis in a series of infinitesimal puffs which create a sound wave.

The faster the vocal cords vibrate, the higher the pitch. The slower they vibrate, the lower the pitch. As a useful point of reference, to sing middle C, the vocal cords must vibrate about 256 times per second. To sing the A above middle C they must vibrate at around 440 times per second.

Because the vocal folds are attached front and back to the thyroid and arytenoids cartilages, which are in turn connected to muscle tissue, they can be stretched out by tensile adjustment in the laryngeal musculature making them longer, thinner and more tense. When this happens, like all elastic objects which are tightened, they vibrate at a higher frequency which produces a higher sound or pitch. Conversely, an alternative adjustment of the laryngeal musculature causes the vocal folds to slacken, so that they become shorter, thicker and more lax. When this happens, like all elastic objects which are relaxed, they vibrate at a lower frequency and the consequent sound of the voice deepens in pitch.

In establishing a component system of intuitive vocal analysis, the first physiologically generated component of perceivable acoustic sound which we can identify as being present in a person's voice is therefore the pitch, also referred to as the note or the tone.

Component Two: Pitch fluctuation

> The pitch of the voice sustains more or less constancy or fluctuation in a given time. This is determined by the shifting frequencies of vocal cord vibration.

During vibration, the vocal cords may not remain absolutely constant in their speed of vibration over a given time and consequently they may produce a pitch fluctuation.

There are two components to this pitch fluctuation: interval distance and time. Interval distance is the magnitude of the pitch fluctuation. For example, a voice which fluctuates from a vibrational frequency of 440 to 450 times per second makes a pitch fluctuation across a tiny interval from the A above middle C on a piano to a sound not even high enough to sound the A-sharp above it. A voice meanwhile which fluctuates from 440 to 493 times per second makes a pitch fluctuation across a large interval equivalent to going from the A above middle C on the piano to the B above it. The term 'interval' thereby denotes the magnitude of the frequency jump between two specific notes or pitches.

The next factor, time, is the speed with which the fluctuations are made. A very slow alternation between 440 times per second, which is the A above middle C on the piano, and 450 times per second, which does not have a note on the piano, may well sound 'out of tune' to a listener. But if the same inconsistency is quickened it may sound like a very professional singing voice. Indeed, very fast fluctuations in vocal cord vibration over a very small pitch interval constitutes what is known as vibrato, that deliberate flutter which is heard in the classical European voice. If a singer produces such pitch fluctuations too slowly, or takes them across too great a pitch interval, the skill of the vibrato turns into what we hear as untuneful singing.

The second vocal component parameter which we can identify within the human voice then is pitch fluctuation which under certain conditions would be referred to as vibrato and under others may be called inconsistency or untunefulness. However, what is heard as pleasant and unpleasant, as an acceptable interval and an unacceptable interval, is culturally determined.

Component Three: Loudness

The human voice is perceived on a spectrum of loudness from quiet through moderate to loud. Loudness is determined by how hard the two vocal cords contact each other during vibration which is in turn primarily determined by the pressure of breath released from the lungs.

Increased pressure of breath expelled from the lungs draws the vocal folds together with a greater force causing them to hit each other with higher impact. Decreased air pressure, meanwhile, draws the folds together with less force, causing them to hit each other with low impact. We witness this concept when watching or listening to a pair of drawn curtains flap together during a high wind. As the pressure of the wind against the curtains increases so they flap together with greater impact, giving off a louder sound. Conversely, as the wind dies down, the curtains hit one another more gently, making the sound softer.

To increase the air pressure and therefore the loudness, we increase the contractile power of the muscles around the torso. To decrease pressure and loudness we ease off the muscular contraction.

The third vocal component which we can identify in a human voice then is loudness which results from increased air pressure.

Component Four: Glottal attack

The voice is perceived as having greater or lesser attack, determined by the impact under which the vocal folds come together during phonation.

Unlike curtains, the vocal cords are not only reliant upon the wind from the lungs for their movement as they are connected to muscles which are fed by nerves. It is therefore possible to vary the impact of vocal cord contact without major changes in air pressure, increasing and decreasing vocal cord impact, creating sounds with varying degrees of glottal attack whilst maintaining a constant loudness.

The fourth component parameter of vocal sound which we can identify is therefore glottal attack, determined by the impact of vocal fold contact.

Component Five: Free air

The quality of the voice is perceived as being more or less breathy or airy, perceived on a spectrum from none through moderate to high and determined by the volume or quantity of air flowing through the glottis.

Although the vocal cords are opening and closing very quickly, they may not push tightly together when they close. If the vocal cords are closed, but are not kept pushed together tightly, then even during their closed phase, air can pass through the folds in the form of a trickle or a seepage. When this happens the voice has a certain breathiness which is described as a voice rich in free air. A voice may also be rich in free air if the glottis is enlarged during vocal cord vibration.

The fifth component of the voice is therefore free air which is perceived on a spectrum from little through moderate to high.

Component Six: Disruption

The human voice may or may not be to some degree disrupted, that is broken or sporadically interrupted in a way which appears to interfere with the continuity of the tone. This can be caused by friction or uneven contact between the vocal folds, by other tissue structures coming into contact with the vocal cords during vibration or by intermittent silence breaking up the tone.

We have so far assumed that during vocalisation the vocal folds are drawn together so as to meet flush and smooth along their vibrating edge, preventing air from escaping other than during their rhythmic opening, and thereby producing a clear tone. However, under certain circumstances, not only may the vocal folds not meet under enough pressure to prevent air escaping, but the vocal folds may crash together unevenly, their edges being corrugated and uneven, rubbing against each other and producing a sound which sounds broken, frictional, rough and discontinuous. These broken sounds are referred to as disrupted.

At other times, such as during laryngitis or influenza or when the vocal cords are damaged, the vocal tone may be intermittently broken with silences. In addition, other tissue structures in the larynx may come into contact with the vocal cords during vocalisation, interrupting the tone.

The sixth vocal component parameter which we can identify within the human voice is therefore disruption.

Component Seven: Register

The voice is produced with what is perceived as a certain register, either modal, falsetto, whistle or vocal fry. The voice can also be perceived as being composed of a blended combination of modal and falsetto.

If a person begins to sing the lowest note possible and rises one note at a time up to the highest he or she can sing, it will be possible to discern alterations in the timbre at certain points, as though the person has 'changed voices'. Among the changes which a listener would observe would be a shift of 'register'.

Most voices have two main registers in singing, known as modal and falsetto. The most familiar and easily recognisable changes between the modal and falsetto registers occurs when a man or a woman ascends upwards from a deep pitch towards higher ones during which at a certain point a 'register break' occurs where the voice 'breaks' out of modal and into falsetto. It is this register break which is exaggerated and musicalised in the yodelling style of singing originating in Switzerland. In classical European singing, singers learn to blend the two registers together so that the break is not heard.

Scientific instrumentational investigation has not yet been able to explain exactly what does cause the audible shifts in timbre which give rise to particular registers. We do know, however, that the alterations in the size of the glottis are instrumental in effecting change in what is known as voice register.

Both modal and falsetto register can be produced on low and high pitches, though the higher the voice in pitch the more natural and easier it is to produce falsetto and the lower the pitch of the voice the more natural and easier it is to produce modal. In addition, through precise control of the laryngeal musculature, a vocal sound can be produced which blends together the two registers into a single quality.

If the vocal folds remain closed along the majority of their length so that only a minimal portion is vibrating, making a tiny glottis, the voice quality produced is like a piercing scream and is known as the whistle register. Because this requires extreme tension in the vocal folds, the pitch of the whistle register is always very high. If, in contradistinction, the vocal folds are very lax and their entire length is vibrating then the quality of voice often produced is like a low, airy grumble known as the vocal fry register which, due to the lack of tension in the folds, is always produced on low notes.

The seventh component to vocal sound which we can therefore identify is vocal register, of which the two main ones are modal and falsetto with two less frequently heard registers named whistle and vocal fry.

Component Eight: Violin

> The human voice may be heard as possessing a spectral degree of nasal resonance from none through moderate to high. When nasal resonance is severely inhibited or blocked, the sound may metaphorically be described as lacking in violin; when nasal resonance is full, the voice may be described as possessing a high degree of violin.

Some of the sound wave created by the vibrating vocal cords may pass through the nasal passage which runs from the oro-pharynx up above the roof of the mouth and out through the nose, and the amount of air which passes through this tract influences the vocal quality. The passage of air through the nasal tube can be controlled by the raising and lowering of the soft palate which closes and opens the port of entry to the nasal tract. At one extreme, the movement of air through this passage can be completely prevented and at the other, the maximum amount of air capable of passing

through this port can travel through the nasal passages and out of the nose. Between these two extremes, an entire spectrum of nasal air flow is possible.

When the soft palate is lowered, allowing maximum nasal resonance, the voice is described as possessing a lot of violin. When the soft palate is closed so that nasal resonance is inhibited, the voice is described as lacking in violin.

The eighth vocal component of the human voice which we can identify is therefore the degree of nasal resonance which is given the instrumental and metaphorical name of violin and perceived on a spectrum from none through moderate to high.

Component Nine: Harmonic resonance – Flute, Clarinet, Saxophone

Harmonic timbre is the particular quality of the voice determined by the shape and dimensions of the vocal tract or voice tube. Harmonic timbre may be arbitrarily divided into three qualities arising from a short narrow tract, a medium length and diameter tract and a fully lengthened and dilated tract. These are given the names 'Flute', 'Clarinet' and 'Saxophone' respectively.

The vocal tract which runs upwards from the larynx, becomes the pharynx, turns into the oro-pharynx and curls round to become the mouth is capable of altering its size and shape. And it is the shape and movement of this tube which governs so much of the specific quality of a voice which we hear, regardless of the degree and combination of the eight component parameters hitherto identified.

To understand how the movement and configuration of this tube affects vocal quality it will be useful to imagine three crude tubes, closed at the bottom but open at the top, all made of exactly the same substance but constructed to different diameters and different lengths. The first is short and narrow; the second is relatively longer and wider; and the third is much longer and more dilated again. Imagine that we hold a tuning fork which produces middle C over the top of each tube in turn and listen to the sound of the note echoing or resonating inside the tubes. In moving from listening to the sound inside the first tube to the same note echoing or resonating in the second and then the third, the listener would hear a change of timbre. Probably, the first tube would sound more comparable to a flute, the second tube would sound more comparable to the clarinet, whilst the sound produced by the third tube would sound more akin to the saxophone; they would all however sound the note C.

With regard to voice production, both the length and the diameter of the voice tube or vocal tract can alter, producing a variety of timbres, yet the pitch can be held constant by an unchanging frequency of vocal cord vibration. So, imagine that instead of a tuning fork at the top of three crude tubes, you have vibrating vocal cords at the bottom of one tube which can change its length and diameter to assume the relative dimensions of all three tubes. This gives some idea of how different timbres are created by the vocal instrument.

The vocal tract which runs downwards from the lips to the larynx is an elastic tube which can assume various lengths and diameters.

In place of the three crude tubes, we can now therefore pinpoint three arbitrary degrees of dilation and lengthening along the path of the vocal tract. The first compares to a flute-like tube, whereby the larynx is high in the neck and the tract is quite constricted creating a short, narrow tube, such as when we blow a kiss or whistle. The second configuration, which compares to the clarinet-like tube, is characterised by a lower position of the larynx in the neck creating a longer tube which is more dilated, such as when we steam up a pair of glasses. The third configuration, which compares to the saxophone-like tube, is characterised by a complete descent of the larynx in the neck, creating a long tube with maximum dilation, such as when we yawn.

If the vibratory frequency of the vocal cords is maintained at a constant, say at 256 times per second, producing middle C, whilst the vocal tract moves from Flute Configuration through Clarinet Configuration to Saxophone Configuration, the effect will be to sing the same note with three very distinct timbres, comparable to that achieved when playing the note C on a tuning fork held above the three separate crude tubes imagined earlier.

In Voice Movement Therapy, we give the vocal timbre produced by a short narrow voice tube the instrumental name Flute Timbre; we name the vocal timbre produced by a medium length and diameter tube Clarinet Timbre; and we call the vocal timbre produced by a fully lengthened and dilated voice tube Saxophone Timbre.

Component Ten: Articulation

The human voice may be perceived as producing sounds which appear close to a sound usable within the spoken language of a particular culture and which are produced by the shapes of the vocal tract in combination with the movements of tongue and lips.

It is the harmonic embellishment of a pitch caused by changing dimensions of the vocal tract which gives rise to specific timbres which we call vowels and which are born from very specific shapes of the vocal tract.

In addition, the air flow from the larynx may be momentarily stopped. Sometimes the air is stopped at the back of the mouth, such as when we say 'k'. Other consonants are produced by interrupting the air flow at the lips, such as 'p' or 'b'. Some articulate sounds are used in one language but not in another. For example, 'ach' is used in German and Arabic but not in English.

The tenth and last vocal component or parameter is therefore articulation, composed of vowels and consonants.

The System of Ten Vocal Components

From a simple understanding of vocal physiology it is therefore possible to deduce ten elements which combine to form the sound of the human voice. When listening to a person vocalising, whether in song, or in speech, whether in a therapeutic or a creative context, a practitioner can be trained to listen to the voice in terms of these components which provide the basis for interpretation, analysis and training. These components of vocal expression form the core of a system of Voicework which is both an analytic profile for interpreting voices, a psychotherapeutic means by which to investigate the way psychological material is communicated through specific vocal qualities, a training system for developing the expressiveness of voices and a physiotherapeutic means by which to release the voice from functional misuse.

I have presented extensive recordings of the ten vocal components with a detailed explanation of the Voice Movement Therapy System of Vocal Analysis on a set of audio tapes, *The Singing Cure: Liberating Self Expression Through Voice Movement Therapy* (Newham 1998).

To recap, here are the ten components:

Component One: Pitch

Each vocal sound is perceived to have a certain pitch, note or fundamental tone, determined by the frequency of vocal cord vibration. This is perceived within the metaphor of high to low, though in fact it does not relate to spatial dimensions but to speed of vibration in time.

Component Two: Pitch fluctuation

The pitch of the voice sustains more or less constancy or fluctuation in a given time. This is determined by the shifting frequencies of vocal cord vibration.

Component Three: Loudness

The human voice is perceived on a spectrum of loudness from quiet through moderate to loud. Loudness is determined by how hard the two vocal cords contact each other during vibration which is in turn primarily determined by the pressure of breath released from the lungs.

Component Four: Glottal attack

The voice is perceived as having greater or lesser attack, determined by the impact under which the vocal folds come together during phonation.

Component Five: Free air

The quality of the voice is perceived as being more or less breathy or airy, perceived on a spectrum from none through moderate to high and determined by the volume or quantity of air flowing through the glottis.

Component Six: Disruption

The human voice may or may not be to some degree disrupted, that is broken or sporadically interrupted in a way which appears to interfere with the continuity of the tone. This can be caused by friction or uneven contact between the vocal folds, by other tissue structures coming into contact with the vocal cords during vibration or by intermittent silence breaking up the tone.

Component Seven: Register

The voice is produced with what is perceived as a certain register, either modal, falsetto, whistle or vocal fry. The voice can also be perceived as being composed of a blended combination of modal and falsetto.

Component Eight: Violin

The human voice may be heard as possessing a spectral degree of nasal resonance from none through moderate to high. When nasal resonance is severely inhibited or blocked, the sound may metaphorically be described as lacking in violin; when nasal resonance is full, the voice may be described as possessing a high degree of violin.

Component Nine: Harmonic resonance – Flute, Clarinet, Saxophone

Harmonic timbre is the particular quality of the voice determined by the shape and dimensions of the vocal tract or voice tube. Harmonic timbre may be arbitrarily divided into three qualities arising from a short narrow tract, a medium length and diameter tract and a fully lengthened and dilated tract. These are given the names 'Flute', 'Clarinet' and 'Saxophone' respectively.

Component Ten: Articulation

The human voice may be perceived as producing sounds which appear close to a sound usable within the spoken language of a particular culture and which are produced by the shapes of the vocal tract in combination with the movements of tongue and lips.

Further Information

For further information including a list of qualified Voice Movement Therapy practitioners, a full prospectus of trainings and courses and a complete list of currently available resources including the accompanying video and set of audio tapes, please contact:

The Administrator
Voice Movement Therapy
PO Box 4218
London
SE22 0JE
Tel: (+44) (0) 181 693 9502
Fax: (+44) (0) 181 299 6127
Email: info@voicework.com

Information can also be accessed on the Voice Movement Therapy web site: www.voicework.com

References

Freud, S. (1953–74) *Standard Edition of the Complete Psychological Works of Sigmund Freud*, Volume 2, edited by James Strachey in collaboration with Anna Freud, assisted by Alix Strachey and Alan Tyson. London: Hogarth Press and the Institute of Psychoanalysis.

Newham, P. (1997a) *Shouting for Jericho: The Work of Paul Newham on the Human Voice*. Video. London: Tigers Eye/Class Productions.

Newham, P. (1997b) *Therapeutic Voicework: Principles and Practice for the Use of Singing as a Therapy*. London: Jessica Kingsley Publishers.

Newham. P. (1998) *The Singing Cure: Liberating Self Expression Through Voice Movement Therapy*. Audio cassettes. Boulder: Sounds True.

Newham, P. (1999) *Using Voice and Movement in Therapy: The Practical Application of Voice Movement Therapy*. London: Jessica Kingsley Publishers.

Index